HOW TO INFLUENCE PEOPLE

*Develop Positive Thinking And Mindset For Success,
Improve Your Decision-making And Communication
Skills by Making Room For Emotional Intelligence And
Learn,*

How to Influence People a Beginners Guide.

AUTHOR:

BRANDON FILIP, PETER COOPER

TABLE OF CONTENTS

Introduction 1

Chapter One 5

Introduction to Psychology........................... 5

    Overview of Psychology 5

    Psychology Disciplines...9

    Key Questions of Psychology 13

    Why Learn Psychology...17

Chapter Two...22

Social Psychology...22

    What is Social Psychology?....................................22

    Aspects of Social Psychology 26

    Social Influence 30

    How to Become a Social Psychologist................33

Chapter Three 39

Psychology And The Brain 39

    Studying The Brain 39

    The Brain And Nervous System...........................43

    Neurons..47

    Synapses 50

    Hormones And Behavior 56

Chapter Four **62**

Understanding The World Around us **62**

Sensation And Perception 62

Learning And Conditioning 65

Attention 67

Intelligence 69

State of Consciousness...71

Chapter Five **75**

Memory **75**

Overview of Memory...75

Using The Memory..77

The Stages of Memory 80

Organization of Memory 84

When Memory Fails 87

How to Boost Your Memory..90

Chapter Six **96**

Psychological Disorder **96**

Introduction...96

What Psychological Disorder is? 98

How psychological Disorder Are Diagnosed 101

Types of Psychological Disorder.......................................103

Treatments of Psychological Disorder Disorder..............110

Conclusion **114**

INTRODUCTION

Do you wish to develop positive thinking and mindset for success? Do you nurture the desire to enhance your decision-making and communication skills and thus be known as a person who influences people? Then you are fortunate to lay your hands on one of the best books that are designed to positively transform you in a way you may have never imagined.

To actualize this, you must learn about this vital subject called psychology. But you may be wondering, won't there be a need for me to go to a college or university? If you feel that way, you aren't wrong. After all, in today's world, Psychology is a course studied in several colleges and universities. But does that mean that psychology, as a subject, can only be understood when you badge a degree in a reputable institution? The answer is definitely no! Many people who learned about Psychology today only invested in books that serve as an eye-opener in explaining the essential parts of Psychology, and today, they can boast of a reasonable level of understanding of the subject.

To learn about the human mind and behavior, it is not mandatory that you study in a university, in fact, more than ever before, information on this subject is often widespread that everyone who desires to learn about psychology will have their desire come to reality. Yes, you will be thrilled to learn about how you can influence people intelligently with this concept. With a burning desire to pan through what you hope to enjoy, let me take you through the overview.

Your roadway to influencing people wouldn't be obtainable without a proper understanding of Psychology. Then, you will learn about psychology disciplines, some critical questions about Psychology and why the effort to understand psychology is worthwhile. After that, you will learn about social psychology, which is an aspect of Psychology. In this part, you will understand the social influence and skills to possess to be a social psychologist.

The brain is another crucial aspect that will enable you to understand vividly how to influence people. Therefore, I will highlight the brain, the nervous system, neurons, synapses, and hormones and Behaviors. Also, for you to vividly attain the ability to influence people, you are required to learn about the world around you. For those reasons, I've explained fundamental points like sensation and perception, conditioning and learning, attention, intelligence, and states of consciousness.

Further, if the Memory isn't fully understood, it can mar the ability to influence people accurately. Therefore, it is vital that you learn about how the Memory should be used, stages of Memory, organization of Memory, when there exists a failed memory, how to intelligently boost Memory and the implicit and explicit Memory.

Conclusively on this book, there are known psychological disorders today, what are they? How are they being diagnosed? What are the types? And especially what are the available treatment plans for such diseases? This final part will provide satisfying and practical answers to those questions.

All these points highlighted above are excellently explained in the most logical and most straightforward term. You'll agree with me that when anticipating to learn something new, its often useful to start with the basics. Thus, let us begin by examining what Psychology is all about.

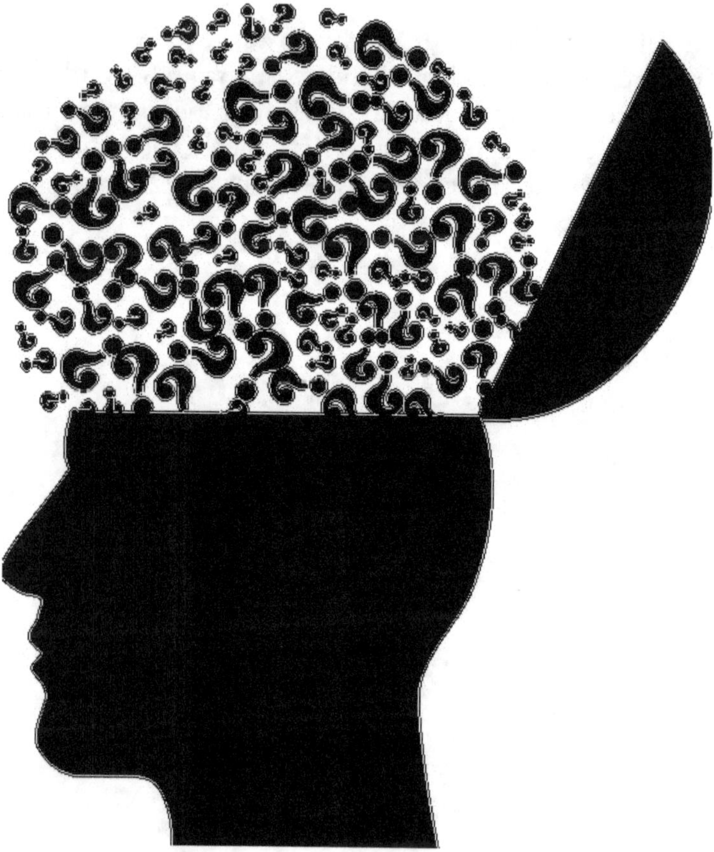

Brandon Filip, Peter Cooper

CHAPTER ONE

INTRODUCTION TO PSYCHOLOGY

Overview of Psychology

When you hear the word psychology, what comes to mind? Probably you'd think of it as a study of the human mind and behavior, which is correct. But is that all there is about psychology? Surely no! Psychology is a broad discipline the entails the study of human development, thought, behavior, motivation, personality, emotion, and so much more. Over the years, it has been discovered that when an individual gain a comprehensive understanding of psychology, such individual will undeniably obtain insight into their behaviors as well as that of the environments - humans inclusive.

Any research into psychology hopes to accomplish the explanation of how people act, think, and feel. It is then not surprising how psychologists all over the world are often charged to study and understand factors that are liable to influence behaviors and thought, which spans from biological influences to social influences. The field of psychology can be applied in several areas. It includes self-help, mental health treatment, personal enhancement, and several other aspects that concern our daily living and health.

Sincerely speaking, to capture all that psychology means in a single definition is complicated, yet, there are known topics like social behaviors, development, feelings and emotions, motivations and that personality that stands for just a portion of what psychology seeks to understand.

Today, there are many misconceptions and confusions about what psychology is all about. For instance, some Tv shows and movies portray psychology is the act of using the human mind to address crimes and accurately predict what a criminal's next movement will be. That's not all; some traditional folks depict it as gray and wise. They see a psychologist as someone who listens to an explanation from clients about their story, the difficult part especially. Regardless of these misconceptions, we are glad that there is one essential truth that keeps standing out in these thoughts shared by most people. Moreover, there are more to those fundamental truths revealed.

It is true today that there are some psychologists that aid in solving crimes, and there are countless numbers of experts who handle mental health issues. Nevertheless, there is an overwhelmingly large number of psychologists that are found in the designing and implementing of public health facilities. For some, they assist in the investigation of computer design, airplane safety, and military issues. Irrespective of where a psychologist is working or discharging his duties, he undeniably has a weighty task to predict, influence, explain, and describe accurately human behavior. But that leads us to an important question, which is How long has psychology been into existence, or how did it come to be in reality.

How Psychology Came to Be

Psychology evolved from both philosophy and biology. And checking these two subjects, we are taken back into the early Greek thinker, which includes Aristotle and Socrates. This knowledge brings us closer to the root of the word "psychology." So, the word psychology is derived and gotten from the Greek word psyche, which, when taken literally, it means "life." But the derivative means "Self." Therefore, the development of psychology as a separate and stand-alone field of knowledge emerges when Wilhelm Wundt instituted his first experimental psychology lab in the year 1879, in Leipzig, Germany.

In his work, Wundt was focused on analyzing the structures that constitute the mind's structures. This viewpoint depends solely on the sensations and feelings via the application of introspection. As a result, Wundt was able to come up with the belief that a properly trained person will never find it hard to identify or correct the mental processes that go hand in hand with feelings, thoughts, and sensations.

With these brief, yet rich history, peer into four leading concepts of psychology that have to be examined because they are so important and imperative.

1. Psychology is Theoretical and an Applied Discipline.

Psychology is identified as both having theoretical and applied Discipline. The research done in Psychology tends to understand and elucidate on how we feel, think, and act. So the research psychologist adds to the understanding of why people operate as they do with the different factors that have an impact on human behavior and mind. It should be known that a large part of psychology is committed to the diagnosis and treatment of mental health problem, general well-being, productivity, ergonomics, and so much more.

2. There are Different Specialty Areas in Psychology. Psychology is a wide and diverse field. And many specialty areas have developed. Check into the following areas of research and application within the sphere of Psychology. I will highlight them and speak broadly on each in the next subheading.

Abnormal Psychology. This involves the study of abnormal behavior and psychopathology. Biological Psychology. This studies how biological processes influence the mind and behavior.

Clinical Psychology. This is focused on the diagnosis, assessment, and treatment of mental disorders. Cognitive Psychology. This aspect is designed on the study of human thoughts, processes, and cognition.

Social Psychology. The is channeled on understanding group behavior as well as social influences that shape how individual behaves.

Personality Psychology. This studies how personalities develop and how the style of actions, thoughts, and characteristics that makes each own unique.

Developmental Psychology. This area checks into human growth and development of lifespan. Comparative Psychology. This entails the study of animal behaviors.

Forensic Psychology. This aspect deals with the study of principles in the criminal and legal justice system.

Industrial-organizational Psychology. This is the adoption of psychological research to improve work performance and handpick employees.

3. Psychology Employs The Use of Scientific Methods. Another aspect of Psychology is the application of objective scientific methods to understand, predict, and explain human behavior. Since its migrating from its roots, it begins to employ scientific methods to study human behavior.

4. There is Varying Application Of Psychology. One of the apparent applications is the field of mental health where psychologists employ research and several findings for clients to manage their psychological distress and illness. In essence, it is used in helping a person live healthier.

As you would have seen, Psychology is a young science, yet it has been useful in its use as a tool to understand human mind and behavior, this new knowledge is added to develop several practical application that will enhance our everyday life.

Apart from these points related, there are several Psychology disciplines, what are they and how do they aid in the reading of human mind and behavior. Let's get to see as you read on.

Psychology Disciplines

To gain a more profound and better understanding of what Psychology is really about. Although some of this aspect has been highlight earlier, as I promised, I will speak more broadly on each so you can have an understanding of the essential elements of psychology disciplines. All these disciplines are used in the study of human mind and behavior.

1. Abnormal Psychology. Have you ever wondered what can be used in solving abnormalities in humans without the use of pills? Just as the name implies, the study of these concept centers on abnormal behaviors or attitudes in mental health. In this Discipline, what research seeks to accomplish is psychological disorders or abnormalities like anxiety, mental illness, depression, post-traumatic stress, and eating disorder. And experts that work in this field are a psychotherapist and other clinical psychologists alongside different types of counselors and therapists. In this field, many professionals work has in hand to achieve the ability to read into a personal abnormal behavior relating to mental health.

2. Educational Psychology. The educational sector isn't excluded when it comes to the Discipline of psychology. Have you ever thought what could be done to the student that have learning problems or say disabilities? This field of Discipline is applied in the student environs. It works toward how a student learns and other educational issues in students. For example, parents that have ward with disabilities in learning, giftedness might be thinking about how they could be helped in solving the puzzle and reading into the root of the problem. This field of study will help teachers and other educators to improve how students, which will enhance the overall performance of the student.

3. Industrial-Organizational Psychology. In a world where every head of a firm or institution craves to know how productivity could be enhanced at the working environment while they keep the resources used at a minimal rate and yet will still accomplish the same outcome. This area of psychological Discipline is extended to the workplace. The

research is highly focused on enhancing productivity at work. It goes even further by improving efficiency, addressing real-world problems, and ensuring that workers are highly motivated. Under this Discipline, there exists a, which is the human factor. This aspect checks into the human-computer relationship to enhance how people work with some specific machines and products. The necessary attention in the style of Discipline is that one's organization will find surely, an effective ways o function and how to understand how people that are found in groups acts and behaves. This aspect has have been found to improve employee's retention.

4. Personality Psychology. This field explains differences in people that brings about our uniqueness. It covers parts like feelings, patterns, and behaviors. These are analyzed individually to gain light into how some personalities develop and the best ways to classify different types of people. In this field of study alone, there are a high number of personality theories that have been developed. For instance, there are theories about humanistic, psychoanalytic, and behaviorist. All these are found in the personal Psychology Discipline.

5. Social Psychology. Have you ever wondered how others influence people's thoughts, feelings, and behaviors? Then, this aspect of psychology discipline is the tool for achieving that. This Discipline helps in closing the gap between psychology and sociology. But how? It does that by analyzing a person in a relationship to the perceived presence of others. But that isn't all about social psychology? It goes further in looking at areas like nonverbal communication, social influence on decision- making and leadership, and social interactions. In a sense, to understand vividly, social behavior, one has to understand keenly what social communication and social perception is all about.

6. Neuropsychology. What makes up this Discipline? If will splits it, what we will have will be neuro and psychology. And that's what it is. It is a combination of Psychology and neurology. This field of Discipline is used or applied to investigate into the Psychological impacts of the nervous system. And in the research process, questions that are often being asked could include how the changing brain chemistry works as a result of injury, hormones, or environmental factors. And how they impact mental health and behavior. This aspect is actually of interest not only in the medical field but also for an individual who seeks to understand how brain functions, and he tries to embark on the journey of influencing people.

So the primary need is to investigate whether an individual will be faced with behavioral problem after being involved in an accident that caused brain injury.

7. Health Psychology. This Discipline is centered around how some Psychological, cultural, and behavioral factors have a contributing factor to one's physical health and illness. This aspect of Psychology enhances healthy attitudes and good work to help avoid and guide against ailments and diseases. Health-related issues can include stress management, nutrition, smoking cessation, and weight management. What they do is to focus on the whole person being attended to. To help check into what changed their health status. Which could range from many factors like medication, education, state, and behaviors that might have an impact on the diseases s person are having?

8. Developmental Psychology. This also comprises of cognitive, social, and emotional changes that occur across the lifespan. This field of Discipline is based on research and aid in the evaluation of intervention programs.

9. Cognitive Psychology. This Discipline or aspects has several topics. They include perception, memory, reasoning, thinking, attention, problem-solving, language, and emotion, which are central to cognitive psychology, and they focus on internal mental states. Which is it firmly believed that this aspect is basically for the research field; some experts employ it for businesses reasons?

10. Sports Psychology. This Discipline helps to understand the relationship between psychological topics and sports. It entails physical activity and exercises. This aspect can be achieved in two ways. One is by using sports psychology to motivate and ensure optimum performance, while others could use this to enhance well-being.

But are there key questions in psychology that have to be answered? Yes, check them below and have an overview.

Key Questions of Psychology

It is often said that when you ask a psychologist a question, what you get in return is a question. Take, for instance, you might ask a psychologist what is intelligence, and the response would be, why would you desire to know?

But frankly speaking, psychologists ask and provide answers to questions. And these questions have a wide range of application. It just ranges from so many topics. From what our mind looks like to the reason why discrimination abounds and just everything that exists in between these two subjects and many more. Even though there are many of their questions, I will only explain the best and the answers to those question. So you see, I am not just going to tell you the questions alone, but I will also provide you with a reply from physiological's end. And this will also assist you in your goal to influence people.

1. What is Intelligence? Why Should We Care? This is one of psychology's big questions. We can trace back the study of intelligence to the early 1900s when many educators back then desire to test out students mental capabilities. That experiment didn't come up with one single definition that can be agreed on. There are several controversies as regard whether intelligence is inherited or not, whether intelligence can be trained, whether intelligence makes a stark difference in your success in life or even whether men or women are smarter. Regardless of all these modern psychologists are reaching an understanding that intelligence is beyond academic knowledge, and any proper definition of what intelligence is must have attributes like practical knowledge, knowledge of others, and self-understanding.

Caring about intelligence is vital as it extends beyond the sphere of the classroom and has the potential to bring richness into our lives and that of others in a relevant way.

2. How do we Make Our Working Memory to Work For us? The term "working memory" refers to a part of our memory system that allows us to store information in "consciousness." data is stored here because you are trying to call to mind what you've learned in the past or what you are just learning. In theory, it is possible to save information there for an unlimited time, but in practice it is impracticable. But the tactics are keeping the data as long as you need or you'd be able to pull it only when you need it. Amazingly, psychologists have three ways to get that done. One is by chunking, another is by encoding for natural retrieving, and the third one is by adopting deep processing.

Chunking- Organizing large amounts of information to a smaller number of units then you will

Encode- you will need to haul the organizational framework that you've created at the time of encoding you will need to use it at a later time.

Deep Processing. Give meaning to what you are trying to remember, the more you do, the more chances you have to remember it. You can even make the words you want to remember into a sentence and memorize them.

3. How Can We Effectively Communicate? If you'd want to have pleasant interactions with other people, we must ensure that we communicate well with them. Spoken or written language isn't just all about communication. It is not merely about what is being said, but it is about how it was presented, that is, spoken. Each time you speak, you must ensure that your point is channeled linearly, that is, there must be connections, one word spoken must lead your listener to grasps what will follow. Your body language is an essential tool for effective communication because it can say more words than you would imagine. When conversing, don't forget to make eye contact, give hands gestures, and make them more ready and willing to make an impression on others.

4. What is The Key to Solving Life's Problem? Some solutions that psychology can solve are the problems we face in our day-to-day living. It could be analyzing the food to cook, checking for the best route to take home, learning to use a new computer, or even fixing a broken object. Whatever it is, psychology is centered on problem-solving. How it could be done first is that you will need to understand the nature of that problem, probably it will require putting things in order so that you can have a clearer picture of the problem. Then next is

keeping an open mind to the possible solutions that exist, in fact, including those that could seem like they are out of reach. And don't be timid to start all over again if, at any rate, your results are hitting any success. So don't' be glued to an answer if you knew it is not correct. But quickly change the root is you discover that there are better ways to analyze it.

5. Why do we Dream? When we dream at times, we might get mystified. We can wake up and become confused, fearful, imbalanced, or even satisfied. Our dreams, of course, stands for unconscious wishes that we are scared to express in real life. Although, in one of the most recent explanations that exist isn't incompatibility with this theory. Because it is now believed by Activation-synthesis model that dreams are stories that are created outside the stochastic simulation that exists in the brain while we sleep. Also, Activation Integration Modulation posits that ideas reflect the activity of regions of the brain active at a specific time as well as the actions of a particular neurotransmitter.

6. How Does Mind to Body Connection Alters Our Emotions? The answer to this question is that our bodily changes follow directly from the perceptions of an appealing fact, and they tagged these physical changes as the emotions. Also, some psychologists like Stanley Schachter suggests that emotions are the products of autonomic arousal and the reaction of another context. Well, the fact that is that none of these theories mentioned are accurate, but psychologists today agree that our emotion is defined by the responses our bodies, with additionally coloring our thoughts about a particular situation give that.

With all these questions and answers provided by psychologists, you will unquestionably believe that psychology is capable of getting us a deeper understanding of life's mysteries and gives us unique secrets to explore for everyday living. To further strengthen your conviction about psychology, check through ten of the good reasons why your stop here is highly beneficial to your general well-being.

Why Learn Psychology

You might not find it hard to come to the understanding of some of the reasons why you have to study psychology after all, right from the introduction, the book has started depicted the positive traits and impressive benefits buried in the study of Psychology. But that's not all. There are still amazing gems hidden in the study of Psychology, and you won't want to give up learning about them.

However, the benefits that will be explained below doesn't make you necessarily work in a psychology-related profession, or does it make you become a major in it. Instead, it is to make you see how your life can be spiced with meaning, and you can attain success in all your endeavors. Here below are to reasons that your reading about Psychology isn't waste either is it a waste of valuable resources.

1. You Can Better Understand Yourself. How well do you know yourself? Can you provide an answer to that question? Okay, if you can't, then learning about psychology is the best and most reasonable step to take. The more you keep learning about psychology, the more you understand how development occurs, how personality is developed, and how some factors like culture and society influence one's behavior. Gaining an excellent understanding of this can give you a broader knowledge about some of the influences that have affected you in life, either positively or negatively.

2. Understand Claims Better. There are so many books, television shows and movies that will present some claims which you will come in contact with. How do you validate those claims in a better way? Psychology is a tool to aid your understanding of research methods. You will highly be a privilege to weed out the fictions from the truths that are abundant in today's entertainment.

3. You, Will, Earn a Better Understanding About The People Around You. How would you understand the motivations and influences that impact someone's behavior? Without an accurate knowledge of Psychology, having this knowledge might be impossible or difficult. And yet, when we can understand better the motive of triggering some actions, we are likely to react either negatively or positively, and we will avoid being used.

4. You, Will, Have Better Communication Skills. There are subject like emotions, language, and body language that psychology discusses which will assist you in fine-tuning your interpersonal communication skills so that you can understand better what sine people are trying to say thus you can understand them better. Naturally, we seek to have this ability. And when you study Psychology well enough, you can enjoy the liberty to understand the person communicating with you. Additionally, you will be able to communicate better with such an individual.

5. You, Will, be Blessed With Critical Thinking Skills. There are many topics like decision-making, problem-solving, and scientific methods that are developed to help you hone your critical thinking skills. After learning about some topics, when faced with a decision, you will surely be able to think critically and come up with the ability to think both critically

and deeply about such issues. Having these skills isn't just a mere skill; it is highly sought after in the works today.

6. You, Will, be Successful In Your Future Ambitions And Careers. Indeed, there are several exciting careers in psychology that you'd desire to explore, and as you study the profession, you can be helped in another profession as well.

Take, for example; understanding human behavior is highly needed if you desire to be a business manager. Having the understanding of a business manager will help you to improve your ability to be a good manager that interacts with employee better and which knows what they think and feel, which in turn will improve productivity.

7. You will Come to Appreciate Human Development at all Levels of Life. If you are raising a child, the challenges that come with child-rearing can make every stage of their growth seems daunting and challenging, but with the knowledge of psychology, you can understand the change and grow throughout their lifespan. It wouldn't only help you with your children but also your aging parent who might, at times, portray the attitude of babies. Additionally, it can shapen personal experiences each DAT as you come in contact with several opportunities as you age.

8. Have a Wide Understanding About Mental Illness. Even though you aren't a psychotherapist, your knowledge of Psychology will aid your understanding of how Psychological condition is being diagnosed. Then you will be in the know on how mental wellness can be improved, how every individual can fight stress, how to boost memory, how to live a healthier life and how to live more happier. All these will surely have a right bearing on understanding mental illness and general well being.

9. It's Fun And Fascinating. How does it feel to be paid and learn? I mean, how would it be like if you are paid to learn a subject. Honestly, that is what the knowledge of psychology does, as you learn about it, you are paid in return, that is, every aspect of the learning brings reward. Either from the astounding optical illusion and the understanding of how the brain works and the length at which people will go in obeying a person of authority, ACH stage is always fantastic and highly amazing. What could even be more surprising that learning how Hunan mind and behavior work?

10. You, Will, Understand Some Related Subject to Psychology. Take, for instance, the study of Psychology extends to biology, philosophy, and physiology, thus if you can have a vivid understanding about the subject, it will help you to have more in-depth knowledge into these related subjects also. How amazing could that be? So if your field is study is relevant to psychology, you will undeniably have the ability to gain a deeper understanding of the subject related to it.

There you go with the basic of psychology, exciting, not so? Fine. You are having explained these fundamentals about psychology. It's time you sit right and enjoy how you can apply that into the development of positive thinking and mindset for success. And to start, we will be starting with social psychology.

CHAPTER TWO

SOCIAL PSYCHOLOGY

What is Social Psychology?

Have you ever imagined what is it that is responsible for shaping our attitude? Have you ever wonder why some seem to be born leaders when in the real sense, they are not? What is the genesis of prejudice, and how can we entirely overcome it? In the world of social psychology, these are mostly big questions that are of keen interest in the subject.

In a real sense, social psychologists resolve issues that have a significant impact on individual health, and one's well being. It also cuts across why some people possess the bully attitude and why a person wouldn't be willing to assist someone in need. But then, how is social psychology defined?

Social psychology is defined as a discipline that employs the scientific method to understand and explain the ways feelings, thoughts, and behavior of an individual can be affected or influenced by the actual, implied or imagined the presence of other human beings. In brief, think social psychology as a way of understanding how a person's behavior o9r attitude is being influenced by the social environment where the particular behavior takes place.

No doubt, you will already know that people around us can impact drastically on the way we act and the choices we make in life. For example, have you ever thought that a decision you made while you were alone would have been a lot different if you were with two or three persons? There is no doubt about it! While that is to be considered, you have to bear in mind that the number of people too will influence the decision you make. Take, for instance; your attitude might be different if you are around close companions instead if you are with supervisors or some colleagues at work.

Interestingly, there are some areas where social psychology hopes to answer. It speaks about group behavior, social perception, aggression, leadership, conformity, nonverbal behavior, and prejudice. It would be a mistaken thought to think that social psychology is just about merely checking int social influences. Having excellent knowledge of social interaction and social perception are keen on understanding social behavior. Which means that the way we view other people and the way we think they view us will have a tremendous impact on the actions and decisions we make. Ponder over this: "How have you sometimes behaved in public, what would you have done if you were home alone? It is very likely that you will answer that at home, you will be vocal and loud, while if you are home, you will be reserved and calm. Why?

You already knew that the people around you with altering your attitudes, perceptions, feelings, and thoughts. So, one of the things that makes a big difference in the decision we make is the presence of others.

Furthermore, it can't be wrong to attribute social psychology as an academic field, yet the studies conducted by social psychologists is of paramount importance to understanding some aspects of wellbeing and mental health. Take, for instance, what research on conformity has resulted in.

The research has provided an in-depth understanding of teenagers. It shows why a teenager can go great lengths to size in with their peers, or social groups, even when it can have the potential to wreak havoc on their wellbeing and health. With this knowledge, psychologists can then develop public health interventions that are crafted to aid teenagers in withstanding the harmful behaviors that they will likely give in to, such as, smoking, using of dangerous substances, and binge drinking.

But you may be wondering, how did people become interested in social psychology? Although the idea of crowd mind and concepts like social facilitation and social loafing have been introduced in the late 1800s, yet research on social psychology began just after world war II. It was the horror of the Holocaust that motivated researchers to study the effects of social influence, obedience, and conformity. They asked questions like: why would many get engaged in such terrible acts? Were they only following orders and tending to social pressure, or were they some forces that made people involve in such attitude. They are providing answers to these questions made it possible for social psychologists to gain a greater understanding of the influence and power of societal impacts like obedience, authority, and compliance.

So, social psychologists were able to reveal how people could show their readiness to obey a public figure. The study has been on, and it is expanding more and more. And learning about the topic adds to our understanding, and it is also fascinating!

While social psychology is a discipline, many could differentiate it from other forms of discipline. For example, some could confuse it with personality psychology, folk wisdom, or even sociology. Why social psychology is different from these areas of study is simply because it uses scientific methods and the empirical research of social happenings.

So, researchers in this field do not just engage in guesswork or simply assuming that this should be this; this should be that they carry out experiments to validate a claim. Additionally, social psychology is also focused on situations-the impact of social environment on attitudes and behaviors. True though, social psychologists do not work in the field of mental health, but the results of their research have a significant impact on how psychologists and mental health professionals to assist them in treating behaviors that are impacted by social factors.

Amazingly, it has experimented that in the field of mental health, they adopt persuasion techniques which are being identified by social psychologists. This encourages people to discard a potentially harmful situation while trying to adopt healthy attitudes.

There is no doubt that social psychology is an incredible aspect of psychology that will aid in the understanding of human behavior and attitude! Even in the news, we hear stories that show that social influence can have a tremendous impact on people's lives. Therefore, understanding this subject is valuable for creating a conducive atmosphere for everyone. You'd indeed agree that I briefly highlighted some of the aspects of social psychology, but this time, let us check into them vividly for an accurate understanding of the subject and to see how we can adopt them.

Aspects of Social Psychology

At this stage, you need not be told that social psychology is a branch of psychology that centers solely on how social influences alters how people in the world today think, act, and feel. Yes, you have known that the way we perceive ourselves plays a vital role in the choices, beliefs, and behaviors that we uphold. Surely, opinions from people also have a bearing on our attitude and the way we view ourselves. However, what are the fundamental concepts of social psychology?

If we realize these key concepts, then we can have in our possessions these benefits. One, you will be able to per into why groups impact our choices, decisions, and actions. Two, we will have a deep appreciation of how our social perceptions influence our interactions with other people. Therefore, below, here are some of the critical aspects of social psychology that plays a significant role in our actions and how we view others.

1. Social Behavior is Goal-Oriented. One of the aspects of social psychology is that it is goal-oriented. Our interactions function as goals and fill in a particular need. Most times, we work efficiently when we have a set goal. And some common goals only requires social connections, the willingness to understand ourselves and others around us better, or even the wish to possess or maintain status. Additionally, it can also aid protection and attracts companions with common goals or that we shared the same common knowledge and desires.

Another critical factor here is that the desire to accomplish these needs are motivating the way people act today. For instance, it is not unusual to see people that seek a romantic relationship; it could be a romantic partner, a desire to understand what is guiding some actions from people and their willingness to gain social status. Regardless of what the situation might be, social psychology is goal oriented.

2.Through The Relationship Between An Individual And Situation Aids to Guess The Outcome. For us to have an understanding of why some people are actively involved in what they are doing, we must have to peer into the situation, the relationship between the two variables, an individual's characteristics and the context. Results have often shown that there are differences in people's attitude when we consider the situation.

As an example, a reserved person who is quiet and is an introvert might turn out to be socially confident if given a leadership role. Also, in groups, different reactions will come up as compared to individual actions when alone. So, there is no question as to the impact environmental and situations play and the strong influence on our behavior and that of others.

As a result of this, we can determine what conclusion we can get in some situation. With that knowledge, you could make a decision smartly and intelligently. Take, for example, to get the best of your employee; you might need to engage them in group discussions so that each one can come up with exciting ideas which will improve work efficiency.

3. A Considerable Number of Time is Needed to Study Social Situations. The social interaction that we have assisted in forming our self-concept and perception. And a brilliant way of building this self-concept it via the reflected appraisal

process. In this process, what we imagine is how other people perceive us or see us. Another method adopted is via social comparison process. This entails that we consider how we contrast or how we view others in our peer group.

Besides, in a few cases, many of us are guilty of raising ourselves higher than every other member of the group, who are even better than us in some unique ways. Also, in some cases, we might shift focus from upward social comparison to downward social comparison where we compare our abilities to those in the same group, but they possess fewer capabilities. So all these validate the fact that we need time to study social situations and authenticate the reality.

4. We Often Analyze And Explain The Attitude of Those Around Us. Ever heard of expectation confirmation? When we tend to neglect attributes and focus on evidence that validates our pre-existing beliefs about others, that is a phen0menon that is called expectation confirmation. This attitude helps in making simple our worldview; additionally, it helps in skewing our perception to has the potential to add to stereotyping.

Take, for instance, and if you require that people act in a certain way, you might start to search for something in their attitude that will help you confirm your belief while at the same time ignoring the facts - the evidence that is at loggerheads with your real opinions. Therefore, that way, we are guilty of analyzing and explaining the attitude of those who are around us.

5. The Belief That a Person's Behavior is The Indicator of Their Personality. This often happens when we infer that the behavior of other people tallies with their personalities or their intentions. In some cases, this doesn't take too much time. Take for instance, if you sight a woman that is helping a woman

to the other side of the road, what would you say about this woman? Most of us will assume that the woman is kind, caring, and tenderly compassionate.

However, the fact that behavior, especially when deliberate can be a valuable tool for information in some cases, isn't the always the yardstick, because, on the other hand, it can be misleading. When you have limited interaction with a person, the attitude we see may be unusual, or it is being caused by a specific situation that is surrounding the action as against the person's original attitude. Remember the woman I mentioned earlier, remember that you are seeing her just only once (you have limited knowledge about her). She might be rendering that act of assistance simply because she was asked to do it - either by employment or from someone of higher authority.

With these five concepts, what can we conclude? The knowledge of social psychology will enrich our understanding of a subject most comprehensively. It will aid you in knowing exactly who you are and those around you. You will hardly make a decision and feel sorry about it since you would have considered all possibilities, and then you will reach a firm conclusion. Therefore, as you learn about how we view people, how they function in groups and how people form attitude, we will no doubt be on the know on how the social relationship has a substantial impact on people's opinion and functions.

Have you ever wondered why some people conform in groups? Then its time we check into what social influence us and how it impact opinions and behavior and ultimately, how it can help you understand people better and achieve success.

Social Influence

It might not be new to you that people conform in groups, they obey people in higher authorities, how the role they play to influence others, also how some people's conformity to peer pressure leads them to commit evils in a bid to obey orders. But what is responsible for these actions? Its social influence. Social influence has been a subject of concern to many psychologists today. They've investigated how it manipulates peoples opinions and behavior. But what definition captures all that social influence is?

Social influence is defined as how an individual change their opinions and action to conform to meet up with the demands of social groups, those in power, social role or a small set of people within a group influencing the majority. It is sporadic that you've not come across what social influence is and its forms every day. A boy might decide to change his behavior so that it conforms with his peers. A widely held opinion of an existing member may influence the decision of new members. Also, we adopt the views of those who are in positions of authority. It is not out of place for an employee to succumb to the wish of his boss even if it's against his desire just for him to please him. But the question that begs for an answer is why so many accept social influence? Why do they dance to their tune?

There are several reasons why people accept social influence, letting it affect their actions and thoughts.

For one, many do that to gain acceptance. It could be the acceptance of the member a person belongs to or the approval of a higher authority. People go that mile to have a sense of belongings and disclose that they have shared interests on a particular subject.

Another reason is to establish cooperation. So when there is a goal that needs to be achieved everyone in the group must endeavor to show a reasonable measure of collaboration so that success·can be made. Therefore, if a person can display a minority impact in a broader group, they can end up persuading that group to work collectively. For example, a single person in charity organizations cannot accomplish the task of picking litters, instead, when they hire new members, they relate to them the importance of improving their community, these ones, in turn, will no doubt, join and thus the intention of that single person comes to realization, as a result of cooperation in view.

Thirdly, when cooperation leads to the conformity of views, group think comes to the picture. As a result, group members agree on a look so that they can accomplish the pursuit of a particular goal. When a specific person objects or rejects the favorite ideas uphold by the member of the group, they tend to deny it, even though it is constructive criticism. This void can impact how a group thinks and their overall performance because of the lack of ability to cross-examine its behavior.

Also, group conformity allows for a sense of cohesion within a society. Take, for example, if there is a law that prohibits violence and theft, this law no doubt will help everyone in the community. Nevertheless, such law established is dependent on the people that are conforming to the norms established by the majority. There is no gainsaying that social influence has a positive influence, yet it comes with negative impacts too.

For example, conformity can hinder new ideas from being erupting. It can affect people's interaction in a group. It can halt questioning and debating an opinion that is well honored in a group. This features well in cults where when an individual criticizes advice welcomed by the majority; they tend to be rejected by peers, the fears of this coming to reality stops them from questioning and would dance to the tune. Further, people are more likely to confirm for two fundamental reasons.

1. Informative social influence. Here, people will be desired to have accurate information, that is when they don't have confidence in their ability. Then they seek knowledge elsewhere so they can have a correct understanding. But if that is not done, and they accept the information like that, the person no doubt will be subjected to social influence.

2. Normative Social Influence. This is an aspect where a person is willing to be recognized in the group, liked and honored by valuing the opinion of other members of the group. Thus they adjust their thinking and attitude. This includes religions, fashion and watching a particular Movie.

Let's briefly check some of the factors that affect conformity. You see, several factors affect a person's rate of conformity.

One is the size of the majority. The size of the majority can influence the conformity rate of the group. This usually occurs with an increase in 1-3.

Cultural Differences. This can also influence conformity. In a region where individualism is highly valued, there is lower conformity. But in an area where collectivism is held, compliance tends to be higher.

Task Difficulty. When a task is challenging to accomplish, an individual would require to consult several help opinion of the majority, and thus, the results will be impacted. Let's highlight briefly how minority influence works.

Minority Influence

Usually, conformity is a result of the reply from the majority, yet, it is possible for individuals in a group to exhibit social influence. And when this happens, we call it minority influence.

This is defined as when a person presents an opinion that is entirely different from what the majority believes to be true. As the idea is different from shat the group originally beliefs, the attention of other members will be attracted to it; then they bend to consider the advantages of the minority.

This breakthrough is as a result of informative influence. So a minority can persuade the majority to revisit their opinions. And if that is accomplished, the process is known as conversion.

Today, what is popularly used in the United States to change the view of the majority is the minority influence.

How to Become a Social Psychologist

For professionals who want to practice this field of study, they might need a license, and the requirements for a license is obtaining a doctorate in psychology. Further, you will go through an internship, a whole professional experience that is not less than 12 months. Finally, an examination for professional practice in psychology is needed. And then you will be a certified social psychologist.

But since your aim isn't to be a certified psychologist, instead, it is for you to develop positive thinking and mindset for success and enhance decision making, can you learn this act outside the university, definitely yes! I'm sure this takes you back to the introduction of the book.

Earlier on you've learned about the importance of being a social psychologist, that importance is so endearing that I know you'd want to know which skill you need to develop for you to be a social psychologist.

Below are five necessary skills to earn you this privilege.

1. Detachment Skills. Are you living in a region where you deal with people that dwell in a challenging environment? Or they have annoying problems? Then it is essential to be careful not to allow personal feelings to influence your view of them and your decision.

To detach yourself, focus on your goal, don't be distracted, always remind yourself of the goals and the plans set out to accomplish your research. Let's say you wanted to decide which employee to be fired and those that will be retained. You might let the background of individuals to play a better part of you, whereas, this wouldn't positively affect your business. Whereas, when you don't push your heart into their background or allowing their problems to alter your personal feelings, you are bound to make a wise decision. All you need to do is to check their skills, how far they've gone, what unique skills they have, do they have skills that are so essential and can't be found anywhere else? When considering these questions, mean business and be frank.

2. Be Open- Minded. If you deal with people of different races, beliefs system, and culture, you shouldn't at any level allow personal biases, prejudice, and subjective opinions influence your decision. Let's go back a bit to the scenario mentioned earlier.

Take, for example, if you aren't in good terms with a particular group of culture, beliefs and races, you might allow being close-minded to influence your criteria for hiring. Instead, be open minded, when interviewing, never let any of these to creep into your decision. Let that stay outside your business and your choice. Don't ever let it affect your choice and how you view others.

3. Communication Skills. This skill is primarily crucial in Psychology. As a social psychologist, you must be able to communicate effectively. And that is how you get can information accurately, process it excellently and come with a better result.

To be an excellent communicator, you must be able to listen and listen well either when interviewing or when enquiring. Your ability to listen, we give you the privilege of gaining more new knowledge, will help you sieve the truth from falsehood and make an informed decision.

Besides, you must learn how to read body language. Hand gestures, facial expressions, and so many other body languages will improve your chances of making an informed decision that is modern and helpful to you and others.

4. Research Skills. One blunt truth is that until we die, there is never going to be an end to research. But how well are analysis being carried out today? Frankly, only a few people are doing it right.

For you, you need understand that conducting research is highly beyond objective and rigorous analysis on your own, preferably, it includes to study, locate, and follow the research that has been undertaken previously by researchers in several fields of study.

This demands that you embrace some of the endearing traits of researchers. They are relentless until they get to the root of their findings- and that will enhance them to influence people. Their open-mindedness and detachment will aid them to get the hard fact and truth and sense when an inevitable result of the research is biased and not relevant nor valid.

5. Presentation Skills. To be able to convince people and learn them think your well, first, you must acknowledge that your research it a tool, that is result gained from your research will be helpful in the course of your presentation.

How you present your argument or your point matters a lot. You need to capture people emotion, make eye contact when showing your results, make it a spontaneous delivery.

Also, ensure that the introduction of your words arouse interests and wants people to hear more. Note, importantly, ensure that these folks are convinced of what you are presenting. The secret to this is that you to be satisfied first, then offering it wouldn't be a problem.

If you have data, graphs, pictures, present them in an appealing style, let it be attractive and let listeners be convinced that you have an organized result to share with them.

Don't go overboard repeating over and over again. Instead, only emphasize that aspect you want listeners to take quick action on. The more they can decode the point demanding urgent attention, you've won their heart, and you've successfully influenced them.

Did you realize that all the traits highlighted are intertwined? Yes! So, you can't leave one and stick with one. All work together. What does that mean? You must worm at having all of them even if you don't have. These traits, being the traits of social psychologists, is also an invaluable trait for everyday living. There's no objection about that.

Furthermore, understanding how the brain works, both ours and others will give one an edge to implement these social psychologists skills. Besides, it will boost how we make our decision. I've designed the next chapter to create a more lucid explanation on that.

CHAPTER THREE

PSYCHOLOGY AND THE BRAIN

Studying The Brain

Everyone living today agrees that the brain is a vital organ in the body. However, only a few understand that it is very complicated. The complexity of the brain demands that psychologists learn and understand the basics about it. The knowledge can aid their understanding of what goes on in the brain when a person puts on a particular action that seems unusual, and they can understand what part of the brain is responsible for such work. Therefore, your willingness to be a make informed decision will not exclude the tour of the brain. Therefore, let's explore this in the most basic forms.

In this section, you will learn about brain complexity. Of course, this isn't going to be a sophisticated check on the brain, but the motivate of reading about the brain is for you to understand well what the brain is all about - the structures and their functions. There are seven parts of the brain that I will highlight. You will get to know the structures and the functions.

1. The Cerebral Cortex. This part functions to bring uniqueness to humans. Distinguishable human traits include thought, human consciousnesses, though, the ability to think, imagine, reason and in fact, language. All these have their origin traced from the Cerebral Cortex. When you look at the brain, what you first see is the cerebral cortex. And it is divided into four lobes of the brain. It has a bump on the surface and groove. The bump and the groove are known as gyrus and sulcus, respectively.

2. The Four Lobes. The origination of the four lobes is the division of the brain into four sections. They are the frontal lobe, parietal lobe, occipital lobe and temporal lobe. All these have been attributed to reasoning and audio perception.

- The Frontal Lobe. This part is located in the front of the brain, and it is being linked with reasoning, expressive language, higher level cognition, and motor skills. Behind the frontal lobe, close to the central sulcus, you will find the motor cortex. This part of the brain accepts information from several lobes of the brain and use the information to carry out body movements. Any damage to the frontal lobe will hinder socialization, risk-taking, sexual activities, and attention.

- The Parietal Lobe. This is located in the middle part of the brain and is identified with processing tactile sensory information like pain, touch, and pressure. Also, a section identified as the somatosensory cortex found in this lobe is beneficial for the processing of the body's senses.

- The Temporal Lobe. You can find this part at the bottom of the brain. And could also be found in the primary auditory cortex. This is highly important for interpreting sounds and language that we hear. Hippocampus, which is a portion of the temporal lobe, is essential for the formation of memories. Any damage to this part will outrightly lead to problems with memory, language and speech recognition, and language skills.

-The Occipital Lobe. This part is found in the back portion of the brain. Its function is interpreting visual stimuli and information. The primary visual cortex is located in the occipital lobe, and it is responsible for receiving and interpreting information from the retinas of one's eyes. Any damages to this part will result in visual problems like inability to identify colors, words and objects.

3. The Brain Stem. Yes, the brain has a stem too, and it comprises of three parts. The Midbrain, medulla and the Midbrain.

_ The Midbrain. Though known as the smallest part of the brain, it functions as the powerhouse for visual and auditory information. It controls so many essential functions, including the eye movement, and body movement.

- The Medulla. This part is located directly above the spinal cord in the lower part of the brain stem, and it controls several other vital autonomic functions like blood p0ressure, breathing and heart rate.

- The Pons. This part connects the medulla to the Cerebellum and services as an essential part in the autonomic functions like stimulating breathing and sleep cycles.

4. The Cerebellum. Some called it the "Little Brain." This part lies over the pons at the back of the brain stem. In the Cerebellum, there you have small lobes, and it receives information from the balance system of the auditory and visual

systems, the sensory nerves and the inner ear. The Cerebellum is investigated to take up 10% of the brain's total size, yet it accounts for over 50% of the total number of neurons that are located in the entire brain. It controls balance, voluntary movements, control posture. This lets different muscle groups act together and generate fluid flow. It also aids in cognitive function like speech.

5. The Thalamus. This part is found above the brainstem. It aids in processing and transmitting sensory and movement information. It takes in sensory information and transmits it to the cerebral cortex. Then the cerebral cortex transmits this information to the thalamus and then sends information to the other systems.

6. The Hypothalamus. This is the grouping of the nuclei that lie along the base of the brain close to the pituitary gland. This part is responsible for the control of emotions, hunger, body temperature regulation, thirst and circadian rhythms.

7. The Limbic System. There at least four structures that make up this part. They include the septal area, the amygdala, the regions of the limbic cortex, the hippocampus. As a whole, they are valuable for learning and memory. Additionally, emotional reactions.

8. The Basal Ganglia. These are a group of large nuclei that surrounds the thalamus. These nuclei are essential in the control of movement.

You will agree with me that the human brain is highly complex. It is an incredible aspect of the human body. With this sneak peek into the mind, you are at a high advantage than someone who doesn't know. For example, this information can help boost how you treat others, understand their behavior and interact with the most brilliantly. Further, we can learn about how the nervous system works and how it improves our ability to understand things better.

The Brain And Nervous System

From the functions discussed earlier, you would have seen the various tasks that the brain serves. For example, it governs how we think and feels, how we remember, the way we talk and our movement. Amazingly, it goes beyond that; it controls things that we are not aware of like our heartbeats and the digestion of the food. As a result, the brain is likened to a central computer that controls all the body's functions. And all other parts of the nervous system is like a network that transfers the signals back and forth from the brain to several parts of the body. One way in which this is being accomplished is through the spinal cord. This part runs from the brain down through the back. The structure contains threadlike nerves that branch out to several organ and body part.

That is why when a message gets into the brain - regardless of where it is coming from, the brain immediately tells the body how to react. A typical example that you are aware of is the touching of a hot stove. When this happens, the nerves in your skin sends a message of pain right to your brain. The brain, in turn, sends a message back to the muscle in your hand to take off your hand quickly. This happens faster than reading about how it happens.

The nervous system is made up of the central nervous system and the peripheral nervous system. For example, the brain and the spinal cord form part of the central nervous system. While the nerves that circulate the entire body forms the peripheral nervous system. The earlier part relates to us the parts of the brain, but now, let's discuss how the nervous system works.

The fundamental workings of the nervous system rely entirely on a lot of tiny cells that are called neurons (more on this part later). The neurons present in the brain are billions. And as many as they are, they have specialized functions and duties they perform. Take, for instance, for the sensory neurons; it sends information from the nose, eyes, ears, skin, and tongue to the brain.

However, for the motor neurons, it transmits messages away from the brain and sends them to the rest of the body. When you think of all the neurons in the body, what comes to mind is the transferring of information to each other via a complex electrochemical process, thus making connections that will affect the way we think, move, behave and learn.

But the question an intelligent person could ask is that, is the nervous system having a connection with a person's intelligence, memory and learning ability? The direct answer is yes. But how does that come to play? Let's find out below. As you read pay attention to how this is even in fact, affects the young children and what could be done to ensure that they maintain a level of brilliance as they grow, which in turn will enhance their decision making.

Memory, Intelligence, and Learning. As human grows and learn, messages begin to travel from one neuron to another one over and over, and each time it does, it creates a connection in the brain. And a closer idea is driving. At first, it takes a high level of concentration, but over time, after several attempts of learning, it then becomes part of us, and perhaps we can even say that it has become our nature. Thus the connection has well being established.

The brain of a young child is highly adaptable. Interestingly, when a part of the adolescent child brain is injured, other parts pick up the action of the lost function. But as we age, it demands more laborious effort for the brain to make a neural connection, and as a result, it can be required to learn new skills or change some settings of behavior pattern. No wonder, it is always encouraged by scientists to keep challenging the brain to master new things and develop new connections. The result? The brain remains active throughout a lifetime.

The memory, however, is indeed a complex function of the brain. In the cortex, there you have the processing of the things we have learned, seen and done. As a result, if we sense that information is highly essential, it is therefore passed inward to other regions of the brain to establish long term storage and retrieval. As these messages travel via the brain, they develop pathways that function as the basis for memory.

Movement. Several parts of the cerebrum as responsible for the movement of different body parts. The right side of the brain controls the movements of the left side of the body, while the left side of the brain controls the movements of the right side of the body. Isn't that amazing? You might even want to reread it, but this example will serve a more valuable purpose. For example, when you press accelerate your car with the right foot, it is the left side of the brain that transfers the message and allow you to accomplish it.

Basic Body Functions. The autonomic nervous system controls several of the body processes. For example, it controls function like shivering, sweating, and digestion. This part of the nervous system is classified into two.

One: The sympathetic nervous system. This prepares the body for sudden stress. This is the part that makes the heart beats faster so that it sends blood quickly to the different components that might need it. Additionally, it helps the adrenal glands at the top of the kidneys to release adrenaline, which is the hormone that gives the necessary power to the muscles for a quick getaway.

The other one which is the parasympathetic nervous system. The function is like the opposite of the sympathetic nervous system what it does prepare the body for rest. Also, it helps the digestive tract to move along so that our collection can take in nutrients front the food we eat.

There's no doubt that the nervous system is an integral part of understanding human behavior. But you can be useful for your brain by doing these following things.

1. Eat Healthy Foods. Healthy foods contain Vitamins and Minerals are essential for the nervous system

2. Exercise. You are required to engage in lots of playtimes. Keep your brain active.

3. Safeguard. When you ride a bike, wear a helmet, or you participate in a sport that requires head protection.

4. Eating Habits. Shun the use of tobacco, drugs and alcohol.

5. Challenge Your Brain. Yes, always engage in challenging activities like reading, puzzling, and lots more. Just give your brain a workout.

Recall that I mention neuron as an essential aspect of the brain, let's take a closer look at what the neuron is and understand how it helps in the understanding of human.

Neurons

Many people today make a mistake to refer to neurons as other cells in the body. Although, while this is so is because Neurons are similar to these other cells. But one fundamental difference is that neurons are designed to transmit information all over the body system. We can then explain that the neuron is defined or identified as the basic building block of the nervous system.

They are responsible for the communication of information in both chemical and electrical forms. Additionally, different types of neurons are specialized in carrying out several tasks in the human body.

For instance, sensory neurons transmit information from the sensory receptor cells all over the body to the brain, why the motor neurons take information from the brain to the muscles of the body. Additionally, inter-neurons are responsible for the communicating of information between different neurons in the body. Now, gain a little understanding of the Neurons in the body system and other cells. I will first like to highlight the similarities between the two and then the difference — first, the similarities.

Neurons and other body cells both have a nucleus that holds genetic information.

Neurons and other body cells are circulated by a membrane that guides the cells

Neurons and other cells have cell bodies that have organelles that support the life of the cell.

Now, to the differences between the two.

Neurons aren't like other body cells that do not stop reproducing after birth; they prevent the reproducing immediately after birth. As a result of that, some parts of the brain possess more neurons at birth than later in life because neurons do not reproduce and will die. Although it is true that neurons do not reproduce in most areas of the brain, yet researchers have shown that new connection forms between neurons throughout the entire life.

Another difference is that neurons have a membrane that is specialized to transmit information to other cells. The axon and dendrites are specialized structures that are designed to send and receive information. The connection between the cells is identified as synapses (the next subheading will give details on that). What is next now is understanding the structure of the neurons.

The Structure of Neurons

The neuron Comprises of three necessary parts. The dendrites, the cell body and the axon. Nevertheless, all neurons differ in size, shape and characteristics depending on the function and role of the neuron. A few Dendritic branches are present in some neurons, while for some, they receive adequate information. Additionally, some neurons have short axons, while others can have long axons. The length of the axons, however, matters, for example, the most prolonged axon in the human body that extends from the end of the spine to the big toe and at an average, it is measured three feet.

But how do neurons send and receive information? For this to be possible, they are required to transmit information both within the neurons and from one particular neuron to another. This process uses electrical signals as well as chemical messengers. The dendrites of neurons must receive information from sensory receptors to other neurons. After that, the information is transmitted to the cell body and right to the axon. As soon as the information gets to the axon, it tracked down to the length of the axon. The transmission of the information from the axon down to the length of it is known as the electrical signal. Once the electrical impulse gets to the end of the axon, the information will without delay be transmitted across the synaptic gap to the dendrites of the adjoining neuron.

At this point, in some cases, the electrical signal can immediately bridge the gap between neurons and continue along its path. But in some cases, neurotransmitters are required for the transmission of information from one neuron to the next one. These neurotransmitters are chemical messengers that are released from the axon terminals to cross the synaptic gap and gets to the receptor sites of other neurons.

These neurotransmitters are an essential part of our daily living, till today, there are more than 100 of chemical messengers that have been identified by scientists. Now we are at the place where we needed most, which is what relevance does the knowledge hold? Below are some of the functions they do to the body.

Acetylcholine. This is related to memory, learning and muscle contractions.

Endorphins. This part is related to emotions and pain perceptions. These are released in response to fear and trauma.

Dopamine. This part is associated with amazing feelings and thoughts.

Thus, if a body has no lack of these chemical messengers, the body fictions the right way and in the best way, but does neurons even help to make a right decision at the cellular level?

For me, I'd say it depend on how you view the word "abstract." Genuinely speaking, neurons aren't smart i

For me, I'd say it depend on how you see the word "abstract." Neurons aren't smart in any way. Although they are complex and there is still more to be learned about neurons. But I'll simplify it for your understanding.

To get an excellent understanding of this concept, I'll like the neuron to the heart. Your heart doesn't decide to beat; rather, it receives the signal and the muscles contract. Put, the heart works as it should. Similarly, the neurons work and do its thing. When the neuron gets a sufficiently strong signal from several sources, then its time to go. Then it sets in motion a chain of events. So the neuron doesn't make a decision, but it only acts out the mechanism. It has no mind; it can't think. Thus a neuron is just a cell.

Synapses

If asked to mention a small gap that occurs at the bottom of s neuron that makes signal transmitted from one neuron to the other one, how would you answer? If your answer is Synapses, then you aren't wrong. But where are they found? They are found where nerve cells join with other nerve Cells. When it comes to brain function, synapses are essential components. When it comes to a matter relating to memory. But what exactly is the role of synapses?

When a nerve signal reaches the end of the neuron, it just cannot go on to the next cell but will trigger the release of the neurotransmitter which will then carry the impulse across the synapse to the next available neurons.

Furthermore, as soon as the nerve impulse has triggered the discharge of neurotransmitters, the chemical messengers will then cross the tiny synaptic gap and will then be taken up by receptors on the surface of the next cell. These receptors behave just like a lock, while the neurotransmitters operate like a key. Additionally, neurotransmitters may bring excitement to the neuron they bind to or inhibit it.

For best understanding, let's view it in this direction. Let's say the nerve signal is the electrical current, and the neurons are like the wires. Synapses, in turn, will be the junction boxes where the connection of the current and electrical appliances take place.

There are parts and types of synapses. The parts are as follow.

1. The presynaptic ending that holds the neurotransmitters

2. The synaptic cleft between the two nerve cells

3. The Postsynaptic end that has receptor sites.

The types of the synapses are as follows namely chemical Synapses and electrical Synapses,

1. Chemical Synapses. This is the first type and in which the electrical activity in the presynaptic neuron triggers the discharge of chemical messengers, which is the neurotransmitters. What the neurotransmitters do in this case

is to diffuse across the synapse and bind to the specialized receptors of the postsynaptic cell. When this occurs, two things are likely to happen. One, it is either the neurotransmitter inhibits or excites the postsynaptic neuron. These two have their duties. For instance, inhibition disallows the propagation of a signal while excitation leads to the triggering of an action potential.

Electrical synapses. This second type has a distinct operation. In it, two neurons are connected by specialized channels that are identified as gap functions. The function of electrical synapses is that it allow electrical signals to travel quickly from the presynaptic cell to the postsynaptic cell. Thereby it will rapidly speed up the transmission of the message. The gap that exists between electrical synapses is smaller than that of chemical synapses.

The particular protein channel that connects the two cells is the one that is responsible for the positive current from the presynaptic neuron, which allows it to flow directly into the postsynaptic cell.

Furthermore, electrical synapses transmit signals much faster when compared to chemical synapses. However, the speed of transmission in chemical synapses can take up some milliseconds, yet in Electrical synapses, it's almost immediately. Also, chemical synapses are either inhibitory or excitatory; electrical synapses are only excitatory.

Moreover, research reveals that electrical synapses can have the advantage of speed, the strength of a signal lessen as it moves from one cell down to another. And as a result of the loss of signal strength, it demands a high and sizeable presynaptic neuron to influence much lesser postsynaptic neurons.

On the other hand, chemical Synapses slowness doesn't influence the transmission of the message as they can send a message void of any loss in signal strength.

Now its time to apply what you've learned. That is it is time to change your brain so aid you think in the best way possible. It is possible to design how your brain works and improve how you behave. Yes, you can develop positive thinking.

Although it takes a lot of discipline and consistency to recoil your brain, only a few people can meet up with the requirement and so do not reap the full advantage. So you need to be hardworking. The fact is that the brain learns and adapts when it is repeated; it does it only when it is repeated. It can reinforce either bad behavior or good behavior. Thereby we have to be careful to feed it with the type of information we need.

These are what you need.

1. Identify New Behavior. If there is a new behavior you needed to learn, pay attention to it. As you do, you are activating the frontal loves if the brain, this will then trigger the engagement of other parts. As you pay attention, your prefrontal cortex is capable of identifying what is essential.

Also, you need to get a bigger purpose to pursue the skills that you need. And that purpose will assist you in stay motivated and continue working on it. Therefore, when you can identify your target, it comes pretty more straightforward to be inclined towards it.

Let's say you want to learn communication skills, focus attention on the importance - to be able to influence people, to be perceived as being intelligent.

2. Work More. It isn't a crime to fantasize about a particular situation. However, the question is, how much time is spent fantasizing, and how much time work is used to accomplish those fantasies? The moment you can discover the new skills you wanted to obtain, think about how you will develop it. The amount of efforts that are placed in that region is needed to activate your brain to create new synaptic connections. As a rule, focus on one skill at a time. When you gain mastery on one, switch to another one.

If you succumb to the wish of introducing several skills will complicate issues and confuse your neurons on which of the connections they should form. So you will need to ask yourself a question like:

How will you get information?

Where will you obtain feedback about how well you are performing?

How do you incorporate this into your schedule?

Will you need a teacher to teach you?

Providing answers to these questions means you are working hard, and that leads to the next effort.

3. Keep Practicing Until You Get it. Begin the actual application of the akill. Ponder over the beat time when your brain will be highly receptive to information. Until at this stage can your brain work the best. Of course, it might not come easy at first. Don't let boredom makes you feel weak, don't be frustrated, don't give up. Even though the practice is indeed the hardest part of learning, learning is vital for transformation. You might need to change the environment to identify when

best your brain works and keep working until your brain gets the signal.

4. Consume More Glucose. When you learn something new, your brain utilizes lots of glucose. Why? Glucose is the primary source of energy for every cell. And you'd remember from the inception that brain has lots of nerve cells, so there are no doubts that it requires glucose to keep it working.

When your learning gets your nerve more active, then it requires more glucose for consumption.

Don't take too much glucose; it kills the nerve cells. For a regular supply of glucose to the brain, always feed on healthy carbohydrates like grains, fruits, and vegetables.

5. Picture The New Behavior at Work. Although many call visualization daydreaming, there is no doubt that it is also a form of daydreaming with a purpose in view.

It is experimented by researchers that are merely imagining a scenes acts to the rewiring if the neurons in the area of the brain that is associated with the task. Also, mental practice is understood to be as effective as physical practice. Doing the two side by side increases your chances of learning and becoming a master of the skill.

Therefore, the skill you want to develop, get a mental picture of you doing the activity. Try to be bright with your imagination. Engage your five senses and do it every day. So, if it were writing you will think you will get better at, you will ensure that you drop into your life what you focus your mind on.

6. Perform the Act Consistently. T this stage where you've finally learned the act, you will discover that it will get better

than when you began. And what it usually took you time to accomplish now, you get it done in a matter of minutes. The question is, what has helped? The simple truth is that consistency has helped you!

To rewire your brain, you must be consistent; you keep using the skills. Even though you've gained mastery over a particular skill, don't stop using it. So keep charging don't just drop them somewhere.

It is true that your brain is powerful, but if it remains idle, it won't benefit you. But you see, they are hungry to work, they can't wait to start working once again.

If you can work with these steps provided above, your brain can master anything you want, don't forget you have plenty of neurons that will be if help to you.

Before you know, people get to know you, they will appreciate you for your effort, and then you can become an expert in that field will several opportunities that will open for you. Do you know the secrets? All you've learned about the brain.

Hormones And Behavior

By definition, hormones are chemical messengers that are being released from the endocrine glands, which then travel through the blood system to impact the nervous system to regulate human behavior. These behaviors include aggression, sex, and even parenting. Yes! No gains are saying that hormones and behavior are closely related.

Hormones influence human behaviors in a large number of ways. And it does that by acting on our brains. Before now, only a few can agree to the point that hormones can have an impact on behavior and not just that specific effects.

But as interests in the knowledge of oxytocin keep growing, many are becoming to realize that it is genuine and that subject is high of interest to a psychologist. Although it has to be noted that the effects of hormones are never simple, but at the primary level, it can be learned.

Hormones are identified as essential messages that exist both within and between the brain and even the body. The endocrine system, which is an example of a nervous system of the body serves as a primary communication system of the body. As discussed earlier, neurotransmitter adopts chemical signals, but the endocrine system doesn't. Instead, it uses hormones. And what are the sources of these hormones? They are gotten from the pancreas, adrenalin glands, gonads, parathyroid, kidneys, fat, and even the heart.

Additionally, the endocrine system functions in large part by acting on neurons in the brain, and this action controls the pituitary gland. Moreover, what the pituitary gland accomplishes is to secrete factors right into the blood that work on the endocrine glands to either lower or increase the production of the hormone. Amazingly, this process is recognized as a feedback loop, aside from that it involves several communication and transmission from the brain to the pituitary down to the endocrine gland then return to the brain.

Sincerely speaking, this system is highly essential for the activation and direction of some necessary behavioral activities. These include sex, emotion, regulations if body functions, growth, energy use and metabolism, reaction to stress, drinking and eating. But something is interesting from this interaction. What could that be you might think?

The way the brain gives a response to hormones reveals that the brain can respond to any signal from the environment and that it is very malleable.

Furthermore, the brain has in its receptors for thyroid hormones, and they are classified into six parts. These six classes of steroid hormones are also identified as being synthesized from cholesterol. They are progestins, androgens, mineralocorticoids, estrogens, and Vitamin D. These receptors that can be seen in selected populations of neurons in the brain and other relevant organs in the body. What then happens afterward is the binding of the thyroid and steroid hormones to receptor proteins which later bind to DNA and serves as a regulation for the genes. The result of this can be a long-lasting change in cellular function and structure.

Also, the brain possesses receptors for several hormones. Take, for instance, leptin, metabolic hormones, insulin, ghrelin and the insulin-like growth factor. What happens next is the taken up of these hormones from the blood and function to influence the neuronal activity and some particular aspects of neuronal structure.

Moreover, in reply to stress and alteration in our biological clocks like day and night circles, hormones get into the blood and transmit to the brain and several organs in the body. Inside the brain, there is an alteration of the production of gene products that join in synaptic neurotransmission and the structure of the brain cells. When this happens, there comes to be a change in the brain circuit and its capacity for neurotransmission for hours to days. And when this occurs, the brain quickly adjusts it function, control and performance of behavior in response to an altered environment.

Although the hormone is vital as an agent for protection and adaptation, they are other types of hormones that don't dance in that isn't found in that circle. For example, stress and stress hormones can influence brain function, which includes the capacity to learn. A longer form of stress can impact the adequate functionality of the brain, but happily, the brain can gain recovery.

Sex hormones are capable of exerting widespread effects on several other functions of the brain, such as mood, memory, attention and motor control. Sex differences go beyond sexual behavior and reproduction, and this affects several brain functions and regions which ranges from stress, feeling pains and tactics for solving cognitive problems. With that, it is also interesting to note that the brain of men and women have more similarities than differences.

With all these said, there isn't a doubt that hormones can influence behavior. With more research, more hormone-behavior are being discovered.

Aren't you thrilled to explore this much about the human brain and several related components? No doubt they have revealed how well we can make decision brilliantly. That isn't alone; they gave us insight into what happens in the brain of others and what happens in our brain each time we carry out a specific attitude.

Although it is should be noted that I didn't delve more in-depth and this isn't all there is about the brain. But the information presented here has given us an in-depth look into the relationship between the brain and Psychology, and how it can help us to influence people excellently.

It is true that in trying to influence people, you must understand what is going on in their brain, yet is it right that you also understand what is happening around them? But how could that be possible! I've crafted answers to those questions in the next chapter. In that chapter, you will learn what it takes to get a clearer picture of your environment. Thus you gain more emotional intelligence and improve your decision-making ability.

CHAPTER FOUR

UNDERSTANDING THE WORLD AROUND US

Sensation And Perception

Sensation And Perception

Sensation and perception play an essential role in how we translate and interpret what goes around our world. While they may look similar, they have a different purpose. For sensation, it refers to the process of sensing our environment via taste, touch, sound, and smell. This information is then sent to our brains unprocessed, then perception takes over, which is the interpreting the sensations and then bring meaning to everything we have around is. Describing the two will allow us to see the role they play in psychology and how senses work together with how they are being interpreted. Let's start with sensation first.

By definition, the sensation is identified as the process whereby our senses compile information and transfer it to the brain. Sensing of information includes room temperature, a distant train, the brightness of the light, the smelling of perfume, and when we hear the conversation. There are some other senses we aren't capable of. For example, we aren't capable of noticing radio waves, microscopic parasite walking in our body, x-rays, and radio waves. And we are only being made to sense what we are capable of. Why? The answer is in the following threshold that will be discussed.

1. Absolute Threshold. This is a point where our sense notices something. That is the softest sound and the slightest touch. Whatever goes below this, isn't notified.

2. Difference Threshold. When we sense a stimulus, we have to identify if the stimulus us changing, But how? The difference threshold handles that. It is the amount of change that is needed to determine that a change has occurred.

3. Signal Detection. This is an act to detect what we want to focus on and ignore every other thing. For example, if you have to focus on something in a crowded room with several people talking.

4. Sensory Adaptation. This is concerned with a stimulus that has remained unaltered for a time when this happens; we want to notice it. Take for instance, when you are you sense a perfume, but after a while, you've stopped seeing, why? They remain unchanged, it has become less sensitive, and you adapted to.

That's for sensation, let's check into perception.

Perception means the interpretation of what we take in via our senses. This makes us unique from animals and even from other persons.

It was being figured out that to translate what the brain receives through senses; the brain organizes the information gotten into the specific group to disallow unwarranted repetition for.

Retaining Constant Perceptual Constancy

It wouldn't make sense if each time an object is altered, we have to process it completely, and fortunately, it doesn't happen that way too. Humans can maintain constancy in the ability to perceive. That in turns make perception constancy to be defined as the ability to see things differently yet we wouldn't have to reinterpret the object's properties.

Now we can sum it up that sensation is identified as the input about the physical world that is established by our sensory receptors and perception is recognized as the process whereby mind organizes, interprets and select sensation. So, if we sense something and there is not interpretation, definitely, there is no point sensing it. How is this applicable in real life? In life, there is both positive and negative perception, which can influence one's success. And what's the key?

Always work on your mind as a garden, weeding out negative perception every day and leaving the flower, the plant to stay. The more you allow negative thoughts to retain, the more negative perception you will have. Therefore, it is essential you change the way you view your life. You have to work harder so you can experience the change. Just keep staying grateful for what you possess. What method, always list out five positive things that work out in your favor every day. You will be expanding your positive perception ability. Our understanding of the world around involves learning. But what is learning and how does it connect with conditioning. Read on to get the answers.

Learning And Conditioning

Our nervous system is also involved in the learning process. But how is it defined, and what are other concepts? Learning, by definition, is an adaptive function by which our nervous system alters concerning stimuli in the environment, thereby bringing a change in our behavioral responses and allowing us to function in our environment.

Initially, the process is established in in the nervous system in a bit to respond to environmental stimuli. As a result, neural pathways cab be strengthened, activated, even pruned, and all these can bring about a change in our behavioral responses.

When it comes to reflexes and instincts, they are innate behaviors. That is, they occur naturally and wouldn't demand to learn. However, learning in turn is an alteration in behavior that results from experience. In the field of behavioral psychology, it involves mainly on measurable behaviors that are learned; instead, if working hard to understand internal states like emotions and attitudes.

But in learning, there are three fundamental aspects, they are classical conditioning, operant conditioning, and observational learning. The first two, classical and operant conditioning, forms if associative learning, their associations are developed between events that happen together. Whereas the third one, observational learning, is learning by observing others. Let's get into details about the three types of learning.

1. Classical Conditioning. Classical conditioning defined as the process whereby we learn to relate stimuli and events that regularly happen together. As a result, we then learn to anticipate what will happen next. Take, for example; some experts have trained animals like do to associate the sound of an object to the presence of food. For instance, Ivan Pavlo was able to condition his dog to identify the relationship between the sound of a bell with the presence of the meal. This was achieved because each time; the dog hears the sound of the bell, what comes to mind is that its time for lunch. So in a sense, that scene makes the dog anticipate for the meal.

Operant Conditioning. This is defined as the learning process in which behaviors are reinforced or punished, thereby strengthening a response. So, any act that is backed up with pleasant consequences is more likely to be repeated, whereas actions that are followed by unpleasant experience are less likely to be repeated. So it merely means that either punishments or rewards can impact behavior.

Observational Learning. This type of learning occurs when a person observes the behavior of others and imitate those behaviors. Even when the reinforcement is void at the time of imitation. For example, it is common for children to learn or imitate adults, so if there is a right attitude that you needed to emulate, applying observational learning to being the best way to achieve it.

Classical conditioning discussed earlier is applicable in everyday life. It is being used both in the therapeutic and advertising industry. In the commercial industry, they often feature attractive models. Thus they apply the principles of associative learning. When an advertisement is viewed with a model, it enhances the rating of a car in contrast to a var without the model being featured.

Attention

In the world of cognitive psychology, attention is a concept that is being studied, and it refers to how we actively process particular information in our environment. Most times, many sensations are going on around us; they demand attention. Unfortunately, our attentional resources aren't limitless; it has boundaries. Therefore, we need to find out how we can experience all these sensations and still lay focus on just one particular thing, and how can we employ the scarce resources at our disposal to make sense of the world around us.

As defined by psychologist experts, attention is defined as taking possessing by the mind, in bright and vivid form out of what may appear to be numerous simultaneously possible objects or lines of thought. Or it could be defined as the withdrawal of some things to deal or pay closer attention to others.

Attention isn't about focusing attention on one particular thing; it also includes ignoring a great deal of fighting for information and stimuli. Attention makes it possible to tune out information, perception, sensation that aren't in correlation with the moment and then focus energy in the information that's is vital.

Additionally, the attentional system offers the ability to focus on something specific in our environment while we send out incoherent details. In some situations, our attention might be centered on a particular thing which will cause us to ignore other things. That is, when we lay focus on something in the environment, we a times miss the several things that are right in front of us. And that is why most time in a room, you will be so engrossed that you won't notice that someone is approaching you or has walked inside the toilet.

But to understand more in-depth how attention works,l and how it influences your perception, you have in mind these few points that I will be highlighting.

1. Attention is Limited. Researchers have found that what influences our ability to stay on a given task include how interested we are in the stimulus and the number of distractions that surround us. Attention is limited when it comes to capacity and duration. So multitasking doesn't work well, because our attention is limited.

2. Attention is Selective. Since it is understood that attention is limited, we need to be selective about what we decide to focus on. We need to be selective in what we attend to. This stage is so fast that we hardly remember that we've neglected what happens in our environment.

3. Attention is a Fundamental Part of The Cognitive System. Attention is even present at birth. This occurs when orienting reflexes help to determine which events in our environment need to be attended to. And right from that stage, the orienting reflex continues to be of immeasurable benefits to us throughout our life span. And helps us to respond to the environment

Understanding this fact about attention enrich our productivity, it stops us from spending more energy on multitasking, instead of focusing on one thing at a time, which will enhance positive thinking and lead to success eventually.

Intelligence

Intelligence is an aspect that is often talk about in psychology, yet, there isn't one specific standard to define what intelligence is. Some have maintained that intelligence is single, others say that it is a general ability, while some still insist that intelligence covers a wide range of aptitudes, talents, and skills. Regardless of the opinions that are being held today, there is consensus agreement about intelligence. They are

Learning. The ability to acquire, retain, and apply knowledge- these are vital parts of learning.

Identify Problems. To put knowledge to use, the likely problems have to be identified and be cared for.

Solve Problem. The output of learning is taking the knowledge and use it to solve the recognized problem.

Intelligence includes various mental abilities like planning, reasoning, logic, and problem-solving.

Also, isn't something we can hear or see or even taste. But we can peer into the result of intelligence. However, a big question cones that are there a way to increase one's intelligence? Fortunately, the answer is yes. Psychologists who figured cognitive training and pharmacological intervention, so the approach to aid the improvement of the brain. There are incredible ways to improve one's intelligence; I'll explain the basic ones.

1. Exercise. Regular. If you want to improve your intelligence, you have to exercise your brain and body. Like a muscle that requires training, your brain does need too. When you use, you are energizing your body, and this can lead to a

wave of energy to your brain. Exercise aids you in concentrating better and making learning more accessible. Therefore, the more you use your brain positively, the more skilled and a great thinker you become. Your ability to focus will be enhanced when you exercise your brain.

2. Meditation. What meditation accomplishes is neuroplasticity. As soon as this I'd launched, the brain can make physiological changes for the better. Additionally, meditation enhances gray and white brain matter. Their functions differ. For example, gray matter is responsible for processing information, while white matter enhances communication skills.

3. Watch Less of no Television. I know this might be a sad fact, but the more relaxed you admit, the better. When you watch television, you think less, and thus you aren't putting your mental power into use. So, if you crave for relaxation, read a book or play a crossword puzzle game.

4. Reading Challenging Selections. Reading improves one's ability to understand and encourage critical thinking. Thus, select more books among the ones that offer aptitude.

Examples of these books include newspapers, classic novel, multi-content periodicals and when you come in contact with new words, check them up in your dictionary or ask an expert who knows and can explain explicitly about the topic.

5. Rest Well. Psychologists hold the widespread belief that ensuring adequate sleep will enhance smartness. It helps one feel revitalized if one gets to bed early and have quality 8 hours rest, waking up will be immersed with productivity and use your brain to the optimal level.

6. Write. You need not be an expert, pick up something you have either seen or read. Doing this will enhance visual stimulations and kinesthetic. Also, practice writing with your nondominant hand to improve both side simulation.

7. Play Video Games. Invest quality times to play new games. Seek for Ines that gives you the ability that will enforce quick thinking abilities. Just like scientists recommend, game Tetris.

8. Invest in Cryptology. Logic puzzle enhances brain intelligence and functioning. The puzzle entails a message written in codes for solving. When continuously played, you will strengthen your simulation ability and relaxing.

State of Consciousness

The separate awareness of your unique sensations, environment, feelings, memories, and thoughts are what consciousness is all about. Consciousness in an individual is always changing. Take, for instance, it is very likely that when you were reading this book, you were focused, but at a point, your consciousness shifted to something you had earlier done with a coworker. It might not stop there, but move to change dramatically from one moment to the next one, but all in all, your experience of it seems effortless.

As you may have realized, it is not all forms of awareness that are similar. Thus there are several states of human consciousness as well as a variety of things that is capable if impacting states of awareness.

Has it ever occur to you that every morning, you always feel energetic, question hypnosis, and even try explaining your dreams? All these are several concepts of how consciousness works. All these briefly mentioned are related to human consciousness, which can be influenced in several ways. There are aspects of consciousness that have been studied by researchers which I will be explaining below.

Body Clocks. Many start their day with full energy, but by midday, it's down. For some, they try to be energetic in the morning with no result, but amazingly, they pick up in the evening. This daily fluctuation of energy levels is identified as circadian rhythm or body's clock. They have a significant impact on consciousness and other Psychological states.

Sleep And Consciousness. There are stages of sleep, namely NREM Stage 1, which is the beginning of the sleep cycle, and it is a relatively light stage of sleep. This stage is considered a transition period that exists between wakefulness and sleep. In stage 2, when a person sleeps, people become less aware of their surroundings, their body temperature drops, and breathing and heart rate become more constant. This stage lasts for an approximate period of 20 minutes. In the stage, folks spend 50% of their total sleep in this stage. In phase 3, the muscle relaxes, blood pressure, and breathing rate drops and deepest sleep happen. In the stage, some experience sleepwalking and tends to occur during sleep. REM stage, which is the final part is the stage where the brain becomes more active, the body becomes relaxed and immobilized, dreams happen, and eyes move rapidly.

Dreams And Consciousness. Dream an entail any images, thoughts, and emotions that are experienced during sleep. It can be either vivid and be filled with unclear and confusing imagery. In summary, you can see the dream as the touchstones of your characters.

Hypnosis And consciousness. The study of hypnosis has been used in several fields, like pain management and weight loss. Many have found hypnosis to be an efficient therapeutic tool. For some, when hypnotized they record that they feel a sense of detachment while for some, they attain a high level of relaxation. And for some, they think that their action occurs outside their conscious volition. And for some, they might be fully aware of carrying out conversations while under hypnosis. But still, hypnosis is used in reducing pain during childbirth, control of pain during a dental procedure, treatment of rheumatoid arthritis.

Drugs, And Consciousness. Psychoactive drugs are used in treating chronic medical conditions. They can pose serious problems and bring about an effect on human consciousness.

Someone who used a psychoactive plant would have his mental state have a higher risk of poisoning. This is because the person taking the substances has no control over the strength of the plant's psychoactive substance.

Accessing these drugs can be detrimental to your health and affect your general well-being.

CHAPTER FIVE

MEMORY

Overview of Memory

In a simple term, Memory is defined as the ability to take information, store it, and recall at a later time when the need arises. But in psychology, the aspect of Memory is broken into three necessary part.

Encoding: This is the process of receiving, processing and combining information

Storage: This entails the creation of a permanent record of the encoded information.

Retrieval. The part deals with the recalling of stored information in response to some cue for utilization in a process.

Sadly, problems can happen at any stage f the process which will lead to amnesia- forgetfulness. Additionally, distractions can hinder humans from encoding information as the onset, or it could be that the information isn't stored correctly, or there is no movement of the information from short term to long term storage and then retrieving information becomes a problem once kept.

Additionally, there are several types of Memory. They are grouped into three.

The sensory Memory. The sensory Memory allows an individual to keep impressions of sensory information after the original stimulus has stopped. A typical example of the sensory Memory is fast-moving lights in the darkness. Let's say you watched traffic rush by at night, what happens? The light appears to leave a trail. And the reason why this happens is because of the iconic Memory. Well, the sensory Memory is not involved in higher cognitive functions like the short, and long term do. Therefore, it is never consciously controlled.

Regardless, the role of the sensory nerve is resent detailed representation of our entire sensory experience to allow the extraction and processing of information by short-term Memory.

Short Term Memory. The short-term Memory is also recognized as working Memory. Astoundingly, it holds only a few items and only last just for a few seconds, say 20 seconds. But interestingly, you can move information from the working Memory to the long term memory through rehearsal. That is an active repetition of something until you can write it down in a place. At the stage where you are trying to rehearse and someone cuts in, it might affect you.

Long Term Memory. Long term memory is described as all the memories we can retain for an extended period that is more than a few seconds. The long term memory involves all we were taught in the first grade and the cloth you wore yesterday. Impressively, long-term has a large and vast storage capacity, and some memories in this storage can stay in our brain til we die.

Apart from these three, there are explicit and implicit Memory that will be discussed later in this chapter. There are also some situations that lead to the failing of the Memory. These situations will be explained, as well as what you can do to boost Memory. Definitely, at the end of this chapter, you must have gotten a more in-depth look into what the Memory is and how the knowledge will help in making the right decision.

Using The Memory

Have you ever been bewildered sighting someone with exceptional memories; you'd notice that they seem to hold in their head encyclopedic storage and remembering becomes pretty easy. In sharp contrast, there exist, the majority of people who can't even recall the name of the person they met a few seconds ago. Given this, those who feel disadvantaged may feel that there is no home. But there is, isn't that a relief, sure it is! So what us the comfort.

The brain can be trained! Yes, just like the way you can strengthen every other muscle in our bodies, we can engage our brain and teach it to remember more and learn any new knowledge faster. Regardless of what the task ahead of you, either the need to study for an exam, or you want to avoid the embarrassment that comes with memory lapses, or even you are trying to learn a new language. It could also be that you want to make your brain stay sharp. To improve your brain, doesn't need a whole lot of rules, it's just simple things we come in contact with every day. These are the best ways to enhance your brain to get the best of its usage. All these that I am about relating at things that would guarantee to prevent memory loss.

1. Sleep after learning. Yes, you have to sleep on it. Ensure that you get a good night's sleep after learning something new. Psychologists agree that not only that sleep doesn't only prevent our brain from forgetting memories, but it also goes beyond by helping us retrieving memories more. It is investigated the rest resets our brain, which is highly critical for memory and learning.

2. Give Your Brain More Oxygen. Our brain depends on oxygen to function well, and for the brain to get, there would be healthy-flow of oxygen to a healthy flow of oxygen-rich blood to our brains. Only when you exercise, you can send in and improve blood flow to the brains.

3. Work on Your Diet. I'm not going to lay down a rule for you, but this should help: healthy healthier. Taking red meat and trans- fat, which are saturated, leads to imperfect memory. It isn't only in your heart's arteries that cholesterol can build up; it can also build up in the brain. And the build-up can damage brain tissue since they are deprived of oxygen-rich blood, which will alter the thinking and memory. So always learn to feed on the Mediterranean diet. These meals consist of vegetables, olive oil, and nuts. All these can improve how you use the brain.

Aside from embracing a healthy lifestyle, which is sleeping, exercise, and healthy eating, you still have to get involved in some other factors that will enhance how you use the memory to favor your performance.

These are memory techniques that will assist you in remembering the essential details of anything you are learning. This mechanics is known as Mnemonics.

Mnemonics is referred to any system that is designed to help the memory. It could be a pattern, ideas, letters, and others. Below are some of the helpful mnemonics that you can apply.

4. Test Common Mnemonics. The standard type of Mnemonics helps you remember words or phrases. One is acronyms. This is forming words into acronyms. Let's say you want to remember a sentence like EGBDF, which is a treble clef in music you could say: Every Good Boy Does Fine will help you to remind you to recall. Music Mnemonics refers to the use of music in providing a pattern for easier remembering. So you can form a song from what is making an effort to remember.

Rhyming Mnemonics. Rhymes are somehow identical to music mnemonics. So use an expression that makes the reminder easier for you. Take, for example, this rhyme, looks the same, cooks the same. This rhyme sends a reminder that when you dice recipes uniformly for even cooking.

Honestly, it takes creativity to come up with memorizing a list this way, but when you do, it will be possible for you to retain words much longer.

5. Share What You Learn. If you teach someone what you learn, show it. It doesn't have to take your through rigorous teaching; rather, it could only just mean that tell someone what you've learned.

Focus your brain on information that is highly needed so you can commit to memory. Now, let's check more vividly the brain system, and then you understand better how these practices work better.

The Stages of Memory

The formation of Memory plays a huge part in our ability to recall information. So let's dig some gems out by expanding further the stages of Memory.

Encoding. This is the process of accepting information, combining information. It is via encoding that information from the outside world gets to the senses of physical and chemical stimuli. When it comes to the putting of the information into the encoding process, we must change the information. When your brain starts to make Memory, this beautiful word is used. When the encoding process is taking place, this is the usual time where memories are lost or improperly formed, thus leaving them incomplete. The function of our brain us to translates what we are experiencing into information, after that the information is stored to help recall later on. The three types of information that we perceive are acoustic, semantic, and visual, and if this isn't complete, the Memory is incomplete. The combination of these three is what aids the recalling of information in the best way.

Take this example; you traveled to a country for the first time. Your visual system develops your Memory of that event- your attention will sure not escape buildings, landscape. The auditory system too, which involves the bells, the alarm system, the horns, and many slots of the machine. It can even include smell which could be gotten from the hotel or a recreational center.

If you then include meaning or any facts into the sensory input, that stage is referred to as semantic encoding. In semantic encoding, what is being accomplished is associating meaning to the information we have in our hands.

Encoding varying types of Memory is utilized in both short-term and long-term memory creation. But this aspect is more critical in the short-term Memory because the encoding is only superficial, and that is why it is easier to forget the information.

Storage. Some years ago, it was believed that memory storage is limited to only a portion of the brain, but new knowledge now shows that memories are stored in different places. And that even when they save, it doesn't matter whether the Memory is short term or long term.

Storage is defined as the creation of a permanent record in the encoded information. This stage comes second to help maintain information over a long period. All the tiny pieces of information are stored in various areas of the brain. The neurons - the nerve cells in the brain sends signals to each other about the information you have perceived. They interact with each other and building two types of connections. It could either be long-lasting connections or short connections. Therefore, neural activity and the strength of the connections are what makes a memory.

The type of Memory where it goes affect how the information is stored though that is, between the short term and long term memory. It was carried out several years ago and investigated that adults can store 5-9 information in their short Memory. And this finding sets to be the standard today, though, the ability to chunk information has given the brain more capacity to store more information, but the long term memory is capable of holding unlimited information. But one may think, the fact that long-term Memory is said to have unlimited storage, why can't we always remember information that we need? This takes us back to encoding. There the information in the Memory may have been incomplete. Also, the hippocampus area of the brain is vital to memory creation and storage. A person who has damaged hippocampus region will always experience amnesia and would struggle to form new memories from that in their lives to the continual living. Furthermore, the hippocampus acts as a funnel or gateway where memories are sorted, and several research has revealed that oxygen levels are essential in hippocampus function. It shouldn't come as a weird surprise that a person with hypoxia would have trouble with Memory, and patients are having Alzheimer's will shoe extensive damage specific to the hippocampus region.

Additionally, short term memory allows your brain to function like a brain's scratchpad. It happens only when your brain stores information temporarily before discarding or transferring it to a long term memory. Take for example, before calling the restaurant about the food you need to eat in the lunch, you save it in your short term memory, but as soon as the delivery is made and you've eaten, you don't need to store the information again, you thereby discard it.

But for long term memory, they wouldn't just let go, instead, stay for a few days or many years. For example how to drive a car, the first date you had with the person you love.

Even though these memories can last for years, yet, they can still weaken with age. And this is because the brain loses brain cells that that is vital to those connections between neurons over time. But just like I hinted earlier, you exercise your brain so it can serve you the way you wanted.

Retrieval. One of the reasons why Memory fails is because we cannot recall it and not that the Memory has been lost. To retrieve or recall a memory, the brain replays or revisits the nerve pathways that were developed when the Memory was formed. Repeatedly, trying to remember information adds strength to the connections in the brain and Memory, and that's why most apply to review note to help them retain information.

Nevertheless, it should be noted that when you retrieve information, it isn't always exactly like you first experienced, and that's because personal awareness of the present situation gets mixed in with the Memory. No wonder people could exhibit false Memory or a change of Memory over time.

Short term memories tend to be sequential, which is why they are fastest to be recalled when they are new. Also, the fact that it frequently refreshes makes it more quickly ignored and forgotten. On the other hand, long-term Memory is strongly linked to the association, and that is why engaging your second sense while creating the Memory often leads to retrieval when the sensor is triggered.

Additionally, recall is also linked to how your brain keeps the Memory. Failure to recall is often the first signal that something may not be right with one's Memory. While it is reasonable to forget some things, it might be time to seek help.

Finally, as you have seen, the three stages are all essential in creating and retrieving the Memory. Although it should be noted that how our brains create and store memories has a connection with the ability to recall them later. It is true that the capacity our brains have for memories is infinite, but we often tag as finite when we have a problem recognizing it. So when there is a problem, we have to think about how to solve it as soon as possible to prevent it from getting worse and avoiding it from being permanent. Before we discuss how to boost Memory, let's check some organization of Memory.

Organization of Memory

The organization of the memory is what makes us able to learn and interact well with the world around us. They can create new memories, recall them when needed are the key to these ability to learn and establish interaction with the world.

Every day, we might lose counts on the number of times we depend on our memory to help function -from recalling, recollecting several passwords and others how the brain works have been a subject of keen interest among cognitive psychology and have attracted the attention of science and philosophy. But how is the brain organized?

As we have learned, memory is identified as the process of used in acquiring, retaining, and recalling the information. And we have discussed the three major processes involved in memory; they are encoding, storage, and retrieval.

Indeed, human memory can preserve and recover information, but this isn't always easier or a smooth process. We might forget or do not even remember information correctly, or they are not adequately stored in the memory the first place.

Fortunately, organizing information in the memory has proven to be an excellent way adopted by many to recall some information stored, to avoid poor encoding and ensure that the information is accurately retrieved for use.

The ability of an individual to access and recall information from long-term memory enables one to enhance these memories to make decisions, solve the problem, and interact with others. While a vivid understanding of how the information is organized in long time memory isn't fully known, we can understand how the memories are being arranged in groups. But how is that being accomplished? It is achieved via clustering.

Clustering entails organizing information in memory into familiar groups. Naturally, memory is clustered into usual groups while recalling from long-term memory. As a result, it makes sense that if you are trying your best to memorize information, when you place similar items into the same groups makes recalling pretty more natural.

The way clustering works is breaking down into smaller groups of related items. You wouldn't try to remember the whole list, but clustering the information into smaller groupings according to their relationship will make it a lot easier to recall.

How to Use Clustering to Remember

Clustering is very useful when trying to recall a long list of information. How will you remember a long grocery list? The best and most logical way is to make the information easier to remember, and that means that you have to cluster. To get that done, you might have to separate clusters for meats, fruits, dairy, vegetables, and grains. I have more examples to aid your understanding. Check them out below.

Table, banana, motorcycle, strawberry, sofa, airplane, apple, grain, plum, grapes, bicycles, lamp, desk.

As you go through the list, it might be that you immediately cluster them into groups already. Furniture, fruits, and means of transportation. Do you think it would be easier to remember all these the way they are presented? That is why you have to reorganize the information and connect each item to a related one, or the same group. When you do, there are high chances that you would remember. Below are some of the clustering method that can aid in the organization of memory. They are ways in which you different clusters.

Hard Clustering. Travel back a little into the above example, sometimes it is either a fruit, or it is not. So in some cases, it is easier to make a distinction. In utilizing hard clustering, you separate items by distinct qualities. Just reason about what makes some items in the list distinct. In the end, you might have leftovers that wouldn't just fit into any category.

Hierarchical Clustering. This type of clustering means that you will have to begin with the items in the group and begin to group them two by two for those that are the most related or familiar. After that, you will now look at the pairs and then arrange the closest pairs so that you can groups of four. However, you can have more than groups of four.

Besides, there are natural types of clustering aside the hard and hierarchical clustering. These are:

1. Temporal Clustering. In this type, you are very likely to remember objects that are placed in neighboring positions on a list. Take, for instance; if the bird is listed after toast, there is a very high tendency of remembering toast after bird if you memorize the list in order.

2. Semantic Clustering. That is recalling similar items from the list. This type results by breakings list into everyday items and then memorizing them in clusters.

Furthermore, using a semantic network model has proven effective in memory organization. This model suggests that specific triggers activate associated memories. A memory of a particular address might trigger memories of related things that have happened in that location.

Down till today, human memory is still a complex process that scientists are progressively learning about. They are investing several resources to ensure better understanding to enhance the quality of those living and ensure effectiveness in their memory. There is no doubt that our memory makes us the person we are; sadly, the process isn't perfect. Therefore, even if we can remember vast information using clustering, be informed that you can still be susceptible to errors and mistakes. So that wouldn't make you overly sad if you couldn't recall information after several successful attempts in the past; therefore, always remember that forgetting is amazingly an everyday event.

This understanding leads us to one basic aspect of memory which is tagged "when memory fails.." in the next subheading, I will expatiate on failing memory and explaining some of the reasons why your memory can fail so that you can avoid that situation and reduce error to the barest minimum.

When Memory Fails

Almost everyone forgets, only that the degree of forgetfulness varies. It surprises me when small details like someone's name is easily forgotten, or an appointment is overlooked - as a result of being forgetful. It has been researched that forgetfulness can happen for several reasons. These reasons include a failure to retrieve the information from a long term memory. Over time, researchers have even shown from their results that time affects memory failure. So it shouldn't come as a surprise is a person who didn't rehearse specific information forgets it.

There are four basic understanding of why we forget information we have sometimes learned in the time past. Explained below are four common reasons why we forget essential information.

1. Retrieval Failure. It might have happened to you that any information you know well has just disappeared in your memory. You know it is there, but you don't seem to retrieve it. That takes us to the first reason why we forget things, which is the inability to recover a memory. One logical explanation for the failure to retrieve information is identified as the decay theory. This theory suggests that a memory trace is created each time a new method is formed. Therefore, over time, these memory traces will start to fade and disappears. Now, if there is no attempt to retrieve the information or rehearsed it, it then becomes lost eventually.

2. Interference. This theory posits that some memories interfere with several other memories. When information is very identical to additional information that was sometimes stored in the memory, there is a high tendency of interference taking place. The basic types are:

Proactive Interference. This occurs when an old memory makes it more challenging to remember a new memory.

Retroactive Interference. This happens when new information interferes with your memory ability to recall previously understood information.

Although interference makes it difficult to recall some things, there are some steps to take to reduce its effect.

Rehearsing is very important and don't toil with it. When you do, you are increasing your likelihood of avoiding memory interference.

3. Failure to Store. In most cases, losing information might ultimately have nothing to do with forgetting. But it has to do with the fact that the information didn't make it to the long term memory. So encoding failure will hinder the information from getting into the long-term memory.

Take, for instance, the experiment that was conducted sometimes in the past. Participants were asked to signifies the correct U.S. penny from the drawings of a group of incorrect pennies. Many were able to remember the shape and color of the penny, but couldn't remember some minor details. And why is that so? It is simply because the only details that are mandatory for the differentiating pennies form several other coins were encoded in the long term memory. But for the minor details, many couldn't memorize it and thus commit it to the memory, in essence, they didn't store it since they feel that the information isn't needed. 'What's the point? Ability to forget sometimes is a result of not even storing in the first place.

4. Motivated Forgetting. In some cases, we actively work to forget some memories. This is especially true about the traumatic event or frightening experiences. Indeed, sad memories can lead to anxiety so times we must eliminate them as soon as possible. To accomplish this, many use these two methods.

Suppression. That is a conscious form of forgetting

Repression An unconscious way of forgetting.

Nevertheless, the concept of repression is not globally accepted by all psychologists. And this is because it is difficult.

Therefore it is difficult to come up with a scientific study of this part.

Furthermore, the ways to strengthen memory is by rehearsing, and it is very likely that traumatic event will be rehearsed. As a result, it will be easier to forget it. Well while forgetting isn't without remedy. The following subheading will explain ways in which we can boost our memory to reduce the amount of information forgotten.

How to Boost Your Memory

Has it ever occurred to you that you forgot where you dropped your keys r you've gone blank when attempting a critical test? In these occasions, no doubt you'd wish you have a memory that didn't fail you then.

Amazingly, several things could be done to boost your brain. Adopting some reminder helps, but how do you ensure that relevant information that has to be cemented in your long-term memory is achieved. This will undoubtedly take ls effort and might require that you engage in minor tweaks or even change study routine.

So, these tried and tested techniques that will be discussed below will let you improve your memory and enhance your ability to recall and increase your retention ability.

1. Stay Focused. Attention is one of the critical components of memory. Therefore for the information, you laid your hands on to be transferred into the long term memory from the short term memory, you have to attend to the information actively. Therefore, when you are actively involved in what you are doing, you are increasing your attention.

With that in mind, a study in a place that is free from distractions or theta can divert your attention. Be it television, music, or even friends. But getting rid of distractions might be highly challenging, but there are ways to avoid distractions. You can isolate yourself for a short time. If you have a work to read on, go inside a quiet room and have some quiet time so that you can focus on your work.

2. Don't Cram. Are you a student or you are a working class who will be delivering a speech at a public event or who will be presenting information to a selected number of people or writing professional exams soon? Is it your custom to study the material in one marathon session? The chances are that if you do, you do well when you-you have to present your speech, write your exam, but what happens after the delivery and exam? They are all gone! There is no doubt that cramming wouldn't make you remember information better than a person who chose another pattern. And what design could be used?

Research has shown that instead of cramming- studying material in one marathon sessions, it is imperative to review the content over several sessions. Doing that will grant you the adequate time to process the information will no doubt be of paramount help to your brain, and will aid better understanding in no time.

And studies have even confirmed that students who study regularly can remember information in sharp contrast to those who crammed.

3. Utilize Mnemonic Devices. Earlier on, we discussed what mnemonic means, and I still believe you'd always remember. But this time around, I'm advising that you utilize mnemonic devices. Some of the tools are positive humor, imagery, and novelty. When these techniques are used, it aids

there ability to recall the information they've studied. Also, its simple application makes it simple for most people to use. For instance, when you want to remember an item, you might need to associate the item or object with an everyday item that you are familiar with.

So often time, you can come up with a joke, song, or even a rhyme so that you can remember a segment of information.

4. Structure The Information And Organize it. From previous knowledge of memory organization, you'd have discovered that information is organized in memory in familiar clusters. Therefore, make good use of that advantage by structuring and organizing the information you want to remember or the material you are studying. It will be beneficial if you group identical concepts and terms. Moreover, you can outline notes and textbooks to help you group related ideas together. Structuring and organizing in this way will quicken your retention and will allow correct encoding, storage, and retrieving.

5. Rehearse And Elaborate. Your information has to leave the short term memory to the long teen memory; that way you can increase the chances of you recalling the information. And elaborative rehearsal is one sure way to encode. How is it carried out? Read the definition of that term and get to read more detailed information of what the term means. Take, for example, the word "dark psychology." You will first have to read the definition of that term. After that, you will need to read detailed information of what that term means; it might even require that you get a book that discusses at length about it. After you must have repeated the process several times, then you'd no notice that recalling the information will be a lot easier for you.

6. Visualization. Many have found great help from visualizing what they are learning or studying. To get that done, never fail to pay attention to the charts, photographs, and several other graphics in your textbooks. If what you are reading doesn't have any visual aid, you can develop yourself. But how? After studying, in your note or on the material, if appropriate, draw charts or figures in the margin provided in your note or on the study material, then use varying colors to group ideas that are related in your study material.

In some cases, creating flashcards of several terms would be needed to recall or solidify some information.

7. Relate New Information to Things Previously Learnt. If you are studying entirely new material, ponder carefully on why that information has relations to what is previously known or understood. That way, you are establishing a relationship between new ideas and the memories you already have. Surprisingly, you would be able to remember the recently learned information.

8. Read Aloud. There is no gainsaying that when you read aloud, you are indirectly increasing your likelihood of boosting your memory. Psychologists have confirmed that when an individual teaches others what he learned, he will undeniably understand the information better and will be able to recall the information. So when you read a piece next time, try your possible best to read aloud, and if you discover that there is someone you can teach that idea to, never hesitate; you are helping yourself greatly.

9. Don't Toss Off Difficult Information. In most textbooks or notes, folks around the world have no problem understanding or remembering the information at the introductory and conclusion of a book? But what has

happened to the information presented in the middle? It is usually tagged as being difficult. Therefore, the most logical way to overcome this problem is by devoting more time rehearsing and paying extra attention to difficult information.

Furthermore, you can restructure the information you've learned for more natural remembrance. Therefore, the next time, you are presented a problematic concept or information, spend quality time to memorizing the information.

10. Alternate Study Routine. Just occasionally, alter your study routine. If you are accustomed to studying in a particular environment or condition, you can decide to shift to a different spot in your next session. As an advice, if you read over the information in the evening, if you sleep on it and wake up the following morning, revisit it, review it, you will be able to recall that information when you do it. When you strategize, you are increasing how effective your memory and improving how you remember from your long-time memory.

Furthermore, don't toil with the help sleep can render; it can help your memory and learning. So when struggling to understand information, get a good night's sleep at the end of the study.

Finally, don't forget to add some fun and even delicious ways to boost your memory. Regularly exercise your mind and body, enjoy quality chocolate, and limit the amount of added sugar in your diet. And with this previously analyzed science-backed approach, your brain health and your memory will be kept in good condition.

No doubt you've got an extensive understanding about the memory in this chapter, but before wrapping if off, I promised to explain the implicit and explicit memory earlier, understanding this will show you why one thing is difficult to understand to remember and why some are easy. Let's head to the next chapter to understand this concept.

CHAPTER SIX

PSYCHOLOGICAL DISORDER

Introduction

In navigating a personal relationship, it is highly rewarding to be sensitive to mental health issues. We have to be concern about our mental health and that of the period around you because that is the only way by which successful interactions can be developed.

Unfortunately today, in the United States alone, 1 in 4 adults are diagnosed to have either one or more psychological Disorder in one given year.

Psychological Disorder is considered the heart of psychology; as a result, if you want to understand some of the basic concepts of human behavior, a knowledge of this is inevitable. But you may wonder? What exactly is a psychological disorder? How is psychological Disorder diagnosed? A psychological disorder is a condition that is characterized by abnormal behaviors, thoughts, and feelings. Then psychopathology is the study of psychological disorders, which includes the causes, treatments, and symptoms. In another term, that word psychopathology can also refer to an exhibition of a psychological disorder. Though, there is hasn't been a widespread agreement on what type of feelings, thoughts, and actions could be tagged abnormal. But some specific pattern of behavior can be easy for identification as being a psychological disorder. Take, for example, a person who claims to hear the voices demons portrays actions that would readily be tagged as being abnormal. How about a person who washes his hands more than 30 times per day? But could the same condition be said of a man was nervous because he was talking to an attractive lady? Or the extreme desire to travel home exhibited by a fresher into the university? Even though these feelings aren't regularly present, they are what could be called as being abnormal. Then, one might want to know what character could actually be dubbed as being abnormal and thus be called psychological Disorder?

The obvious truth to every psychologist is that the definition of psychology has changed over time, and what comprises of Psychological Disorder can be tricky. It is not easy to determine what Psychological Disorder is. Thereby in understanding this concept, you have to understand the exact definition of Disorder. How would you ascertain if something is psychologically wrong about a person or if something is wrong about a person? How would you determine what is normal and what's abnormal?

Look at this, for example, if you were to ascribe Disorder as something outside normalcy, that means some folks who are particularly gifted or exceptional will be considered as being abnormal. And reaching that conclusion will be an error.

Therefore, instead of pay attention to actions that are termed to be outside the statistical norm, psychologists tend to focus on the results of those behaviors and actions. Due to that, activities that are regarded as maladaptive, which leads to significant personal distress are interrupting daily functioning are more likely to be tagged as Disorder.

The people around them also stigmatize people with records of Psychological Disorders. This leads to embarrassment, discrimination, shame, and prejudice against them. As a result of that, the understanding and the treatment procedure have broader implications on daily living if most people today. Today, several health professionals admit that psychological disorders are characterized by both personal distress and impairment in several areas of life.

In this chapter, you will learn more as regards how clinicians define and classify Disorder. Also, this chapter will lay focus on the disorders too. We will review and highlight the significant Psychological disorders and consider their cause and how they are being treated. Let's begin first by defining what psychological Disorder.

What Psychological Disorder is?

One of the most straightforward approaches to understanding what psychological disorders is is to tag an inner experience, behavior, and thoughts, that are unusual, sometimes dangerous and dysfunctional as being a sign of the disorder. Take for instance, if you are single and you asked for a date at your working in place, and you are being rejected, there is no doubt that at a point you will slightly dejected. Everyone will agree that such a feeling will be reasonable. But if after that slight dejection, it transcends to depression, it affects your sleeping and eating pattern, feel worthless, and you are thinking suicide all these feeling s will be typical, it would have deviated from the norm and could serve as symptoms for a psychological disorder. Nevertheless, the fact that a feeling, though, and behavior is atypical or unusual of a person doesn't wholeheartedly suggest that it is disordered.

Also, the cultural violation isn't in itself a convincing mean of identifying the presence of a Psychological disorder because what may be accepted in a land maybe unaccepted in another property. Maintaining eye contact is typical in the United States and Europe, however in some African Cultures, Asian, and Latin-American, looking up to an older adult is considered rude. Therefore depending on the culture, a person's action may be regarded as offensive, appropriate, brazen, or respectful.

Seeing things or hearing things that aren't physically seen, in the United States are an alteration of cultural expectations, and an individual with such experience will be tagged as exhibiting Psychological disorder. Whereas in some culture, such actions will be valued and considered ad normal.

Now with these three theories considered? We still can maintain that there is no globally agreed definition of Psychological disorder, but there exists an influential explanation that can be checked into.

A Psychological disorder can be defined as a regular dysfunctional pattern of emotion, behavior, thought that brings about significant distress, which is termed as being deviant in a person's culture or society. Psychological disorders have much in common with several other medical disorders. In some cases, they might be treated by drugs, and their treatment is often covered by medical insurance. Just like every other medical condition, psychological disorders too have nature, nurture influences.

The American Psychiatric Association (APA) have a formal definition. And in this definition, there are in it harmful dysfunction model. This association agrees that anyone said to have the psychological disorder is said to have any of the following.

1. There are high disturbances in feelings, behaviors, and thoughts. These behavior, ideas, and opinions that are disturbed. These disturbances are troubling and negatively impact those around.

2. The Disturbance Reveals Some Types of Biological, Developmental, and Psychological Dysfunction. For instance, hallucinations experienced in schizophrenia could aptly be identified as a sign of brain abnormalities. So where there exist flaws in the biological, developmental and Psychological mechanism could point out Psychological disorders

3. The Disturbances Yield High Level of distress or disability in a person's life. When a person's inner experiences and behavior leads to distress or causes impairment, then the person could be traced to have Psychological disorder.

4. The disturbances do not indicate they expected or culturally approved to specific events. That disturbance will be socially unacceptable. Some troubles are socially acceptable like seeking for a quiet time to mourn the death of a loved one, in some culture, that action is generally accepted. As a result, it wouldn't be tagged as being a psychological disorder. However, it will be, if such an individual exhibit psychological disorder.

Based on these four definitions, a person behavior can be ascertained either as being possessing some psychological disorder. But remember, there is no single definition that can be used in defining the term; nor is there any globally agreed definition. We can exhibit behavior or inner experience at a point in time, but it calls for the check when it results to disturbances to us and those around us, depicts mental dysfunctional and is linked with other factors. Notwithstanding, what are the types of psychological disorder? The following sub-heading brings us to the answer.

How psychological Disorder Are Diagnosed

How Psychological disorder is classified and diagnosed is highly essential and of great concern for both mental health givers and their patients. While there is no single, one-size fits all definition for a psychological disorder, these have emerged some different classification, and diagnostic criteria have been developed. They use:

Diagnostic and Statistical Manual of Mental Disorders (DSM). These provide a common language and standard rules for the classification of mental disorders. These means are utilized in determining whether a set of behavior or symptoms meet the criteria for diagnosis as a psychological disorder.

This DSM is used by therapists, health insurance companies, drug companies, researchers in both the United States and Canada to validate the type of services that are made available for treating patients that have given symptoms. In 1952, the first edition of the DSM was published, and that was based on the data from psychiatric hospitals and census too. Ever since then, it has been revised five times. The one with significant edition was published in 1994, and an update of that document was developed six years after. The last edition was published in 2013.

Also, The International Classification of Diseases that was published by WHO (World Health Organizations) has been regularly used. And it serves as a guide to fit mental disorders both in Europe and several other parts of the world.

Of course, the attempt of DSM isn't to specify the particular symptoms that are required for a diagnosis. Instead, it uses categories and patients whose symptoms are identical to the description of the class that is said to possess that disorder. For example, they can classify the disorder of mental retardation as either mild, moderate, or chronic.

Each revision of the DSM takes into concern the new knowledge as well as development in cultural behavior that is acceptable about what is identified as a disorder or not.

Because of the fear of social stigma, some may avoid getting a diagnosis. But that shouldn't be a deterrent to getting a diagnosis. Getting a diagnosis is an essential way of acquiring a productive treatment plant. In the diagnostic session, the primary focus wouldn't be to add a label to a problem; the motive is discovering practical solutions, suggesting a treatment plan that is related to the problem.

Therefore, instead of nurturing fear and not willing to pick up a treatment route, the concern should be laid on living a healthy life - one filled with joy and happiness.

Sadly, Psychological prevalence has become more widespread than ever before. Statistics made available for public consumption by the National Institute of Mental Health (NIMH) says that there where an approximate figure of 9.8 million adults in the U.S. that possess severe psychological disorder.

Regardless of what critics say about the categorization techniques, DSM is focused on Western illness. And as a result of that, the majority of insurance companies will not pay for therapy unless the diagnosis is from DSM.

Shall we take a close look a Psychological disorder? In what way you might be asked? Let's explore the types of Psychological disorder that exists.

Types of Psychological Disorder

Even though I won't be listing all the psychological disorders, I will be using the most widely accepted systems for classifying psychological Disorder to list out all the major categories of disorders that are explained in the Diagnostic and Statistical Manual of Mental Disorders (DSM)

1. Neurodevelopmental Disorder. This form of disorders is those that are usually diagnosed during infancy or adolescence. These include:

Intellectual Disability. This originated before the age of 18, and limitations identify it in both adaptive and intellectual functioning.

Global Development Delay: These delays relate to language, speech, cognition, social functioning, and motor skills. These developmental disabilities are for kids that are below the age of five.

Communication Disorders. These are those that influence the ability to detect, use, and understand a language and speech.

Autism Spectrum Disorder. This is identified by the continual withdrawal of social interaction and communication in several facets of life and repeated pattern of behavior

Attention-Deficit Hyperactivity Disorder. Different types of these symptoms have been developed in a person before the age of 12 and would hurt occupational, academic, or social functioning.

2. Bipolar And Related Disorders. This is characterized by shifts in mood and changes in activity and energy levels. The Disorder usually entails experiencing shifts in between elevated feelings and times of depression. They are referred to as either as mania or hypomania.

Mania is characterized by feeling overly excited. These period are identified by feelings of distractions, excessive confidence, irritability. People with this type of Disorder will hurriedly engage in activities that would later leave them with negative consequences.

Depressed Episodes. This is also identified by the feeling of intense guilt, irritability, sadness, and fatigue. During this period, they may feel detached and lose interest from the activities they previously enjoyed and loved. They would experience sleep difficulties and may think of committing suicide.

These two types of Bipolar Disorder can be scary for the person undergoing this condition and those that are around the person.

3. Anxiety Disorders. These are identified with excessive and consistent fear, anxiety, worry, and other related behavioral disturbances. The fear emanates from an emotional

response to the threat, either real or just perceived. The types of anxiety disorders include:

Generalized Anxiety Disorder. This is identified by excessive worry about the daily event. It becomes so extreme that it interferes with a person wellbeing

Agoraphobia. This is characterized by a pronounced fear of a wide range of public places. They fear that they are going to suffer a panic attack in a situation where to escape wouldn't be possible.

Social Anxiety Disorder. This is a relatively common psychological disorder that entails an irrational fear of being watched. It can bring difficult in school performance and other social activities.

Specific Phobia. This is an immense fear of a particular situation in the environment. These entail fear of height or spider. The four main types of specific phobia are: natural events, medical, animals, and situation

Panic Disorder. This is characterized by panic attacks that seem to strike out of the blue with no valid reason at all. People of this such experience preoccupation over the tendency of having a seizure.

Separation Anxiety Disorder. This is a type of anxiety disorder that involves an excessive amount of anxiety that has to do with being separated from attachment figures. This happens most in children when they have a fear of leaving their parents.

4. Trauma And Stress Related Disorders. These disorders involve the exposure to either a stressful or traumatic event.

Acute Stress Disorder. This is the emergence of severe anxiety within one month after being exposed to a traumatic event like war, accidents, and natural disasters.

Adjustment Disorders. This happens as a result of sudden change like job loss, the end of a close relationship, or disappointments. It can affect both young and old. They include a feeling of isolation, anger, depressed mood, and anger.

Post-traumatic Stress Disorder. This can develop after an individual has gone through a stressful life event. They include nightmares, bursts of anger, difficulty concentrating, and several others.

Reactive Attachment Disorder. This can result when children fail to form normal healthy relationships and attachment with adults during their first few years of childhood.

5. Dissociative Disorders. This type of disorders is Psychological disorders that include a dissociation or interruption with regards to consciousness. These type include

Dissociative Amnesia. It involves a temporary loss of Memory as a result of disassociation. It can last for a brief period of years. This is more than mere forgetfulness.

Dissociative Identity Disorder. It involves the presence of two or more different personalities. Each personality has its way of perceiving and interacting with the environment. People with this disorder experience alteration in behavior, emotional response, and consciousness.

Depersonalization Disorder. This happens when a person starts to experience a sense of being outside of one's own body. Those with this Disorder have a sense of unreality and an involuntary detachment from their Memory.

6. Somatic Symptoms And Related Disorder. These are class of Disorder that involve noticeable physical symptoms that may be void of diagnosable physical cause. In this Disorder, there exist strange feelings, behavior, and thoughts that respond to these symptoms.

Types of Disorder may include:

Somatic Symptom Disorder. This deals with a preoccupation with physical symptoms that make it difficult to function normally.

Illness Anxiety Disorder. This is an excessive concern about having an undiagnosed medical condition. Those with this Disorder worry excessively about sensations and body functions. It leads to a change in behavior like avoiding the situation that might pose a risk on health.

Conversion Disorder. It involves experiencing sensory or motor symptoms that lack a compatible neurological or medical explanation. It follows a real physical injury, which then results in an emotional response.

Factitious Disorder. That happens when a person intentionally develops exaggeration or fake symptoms of ailments. They feign illness to attract attention.

7. Feeding And Eating Disorder. This is understood to be an obsessive concern with weight and unhealthy eating pattern that negatively impact physical and mental health. Types of an eating disorder include:

Anorexia Nervosa. This is identified as restrained food consumption that then leads to weight loss and little body weight. They often have a fear of gaining weight.

Bulimia Nervous. It involves binging and the taking of extreme steps to compensate for these binges. The behavior for compensating include excessive exercise, abuse if diurectics.

Rumination Disorder. That is the regurgitating previously eaten food to spit it out or re-swallow. This is common in children or an adult that have developmental delay. Problems like dental decay, malnutrition, esophageal ulcers develop additionally.

Pica. This entails the craving to eat non-good substances. They include dirt, sand, soap, and others. It is most common in children.

Binge Eating Disorder. This includes a series of binge eating where an individual eats an unusually large amount of food over a couple of hours. They overeat and aren't sure whether they have control over their eating pattern.

8. Sleep-Wake Disorder. This is a break in a sleep pattern that leads to distress and influences day time functioning. Examples of these are:

Narcolepsy. This happens when a person experiences a wild desire to sleep.

Insomnia Disorder. This happens when an individual has difficulty getting adequate sleep to help feel restored. It often comes alongside distress and impairment over time.

Hypersomnolence Disorder. This is identified by excessive sleep during the day or an extended sleep during Tue tonight time.

Breathing a related Sleep Disorder. These are those that involve breathing anomalies that entails sleep apnea and chronic snoring that can happen when a person is sleeping.

Parasomnias. This is Disorder like sleepwalking, sleep talking, sleep eating, and others.

Restless Leg Syndrome. This is having an uncomfortable sensation in the legs and irresistible desire to move the length to bring relief from sensation.

9. Disruptive Impulse Control. These impulse-control Disorders are those that involve emotions and behaviors, which leads to harm to oneself or others. Those actions violate the right of others. Types of this Disorder are:

Kleptomania. This entails the inability to control the impulse to steal. They steal what they do not need or with less monetary value. They have the burning desire to steal and feel relieved as soon as they accomplish their mission

Pyromania. People with this Disorder are fascinated with fire, thus endangering oneself and others

Intermittent Explosive Disorder. Short outbursts of anger and violence characterize this in response to annoyance.

Conduct Awareness. This condition is diagnosed in children and anyone below the age of 18 who regularly violate social norms and the right of others. They are aggressive towards people abs animal.

Oppositional Defiant Disorder. It starts before the age of 18. This Disorder includes aggression, anger, and vindictiveness.

10. Subatances- Related and Addictive Disorder. They involve the use and abuse of several substances. They include Alcohol-related disorders, cannabis related Disorder, inhalant use disorder, stimulant use disorder, and tobacco use disorder.

With these list given, if you notice any of the symptoms, it is advisable that you seek appropriate diagnosis, else, these conditions can lead to alteration in daily functioning, work, school, and other essential things.

Treatments of Psychological Disorder Disorder

When it comes to the treatment of psychological Disorder, there is an umbrella term that is used in helping patients overcome distressing thoughts and feelings. This term is known as psychotherapy. Let's start by defining what psychotherapy is

Psychotherapy is the term used in describing the application of psychological methods primarily when based on regular personal interaction, to assist a person to overcome his or her problem in a lovely way. Counseling and therapy are words that can be used interchangeability with the word psychotherapy.

Put, psychology is defined as the treatment between an experienced professional and a client, group, families, and others. The psychological problem that is being solved with the aid psychotherapy is the causes, triggers, influences, or resolutions. The application of psychotherapy has long been in existence. Take, for instance; psychotherapy has been practiced as philosophers, medics, other spiritual practitioner and used in healing people.

The primary aim of psychotherapy is to ensure the exploration of thoughts, behavior, and feelings with the goal of problem-solving or even attaining higher levels of functioning. Psychotherapy aims to boosts the individual's sense of their well being. There are several techniques based experimental relationship-building that psychotherapists use to modify the mental health of a patient.

In the process of psychotherapy, there is a need for the person in question to speak up with a trained professional about how they think, feel and interact with in life, with an ultimate goal of resolving negative symptoms of an emotional or mental health problem

Several forms of psychotherapy use spoken conversation, others, on the other hand, utilizes another form of communication like the written word, artworks, music, storytelling, and others.

Depending on the system, types of symptoms a specific method may be employed. Take, for instance, psychotherapy with children and their parents usually involve play, role play, and drawing.

However, below are common types of psychotherapy.

1. Psychodynamic Therapy. The primary focus is to verify the unconscious content of a client's psyche to alleviate psychic tension. This therapy is briefer.

Humanistic Therapy. This type is majorly concerned with the social context of the development of the individual with keen on subject meaning, a concern for positive growth. This suggests an inherent human capacity to maximize potential.

Behavioral Therapy. These methods lay attention on behavior individually. And it is with combination with thoughts and feelings that might be causing them. Operant conditioning and classical conditioning are examples of behavioral therapy.

Cognitive And Cognitive Behavioral Therapy. This seeks to identify maladaptive cognitions. It combines cognitive therapy and behavioral therapy to carer for maladaptive cognition or dysfunctional behavior.

Group Therapy. This involves treating a small group of patients as a group.

Eclectic Therapy. This is the combination of multiple types of therapies. So it only adopts techniques and theories that work best.

Other Approaches. Eye movement desensitization and reprocessing (EMDR) reduces symptoms for individuals who have gone through severe trauma. Also, body-centered therapies lay attention on the connection between the mind and body to active greater awareness of the physical body an emotions.

Other types of therapist used is Biomedical therapies. This involves the use of medication and pills or undergoing medical procedures to treat Psychological disorders.

The psychotherapy discussed earlier, and the biomedical is used in treating a person entirely from their condition. Although, it has experimented that not all patients will require biomedical therapy, yet, for some individual going through biomedical therapy will help them and will enhance the psychotherapeutic approaches.

The types of Biomedical Therapy are:

1. Pharmacotherapy. This entails the use of medications in biomedical treatment. They are classified into four types: Antipsychotics, antidepressants, hypnoanxiolytics, and anti-cycling agents. Amazingly, the effectiveness is upward 80%.

Electroconvulsive Therapy. This entails the use of electric current to induce the brain to help reduce the effects of certain mental conditions like severe forms of depression.

Psychosurgery. It is also called neurosurgery. This is the neurosurgical treatment of mental illness. It is used for people with depression and obsessive-compulsive Disorder.

CONCLUSION

Conclusion

Realistically, influencing people don't come with no task; it requires several applications of psychological knowledge, and clearly, that is what you've got reading this book. I've spoken extensively on several subjects that can aid and enhance your ability to develop positive thinking and mindset that is charged to accomplishing success. Also, the points discussed in this book would have helped you understand how you can improve your decision-making and communication skills.

In the world today, it is natural to be inclined with folks that have a strong ability to convince people intelligently. This isn't done to exploit their fellow men. However, it is done to educate and help people see things from a modern perspective. They have viewpoints that correlate with facts and advanced research.

All these points highlighted from the explanation of what psychology is to a critical aspect of social psychology, social influence, to the explanatory explanation on the brain, how you can understand the world around you and I did go further to discuss at length what is memory, and finally I revealed what psychological disorder is all about.

There is no gain-saying that you are fully armed to take control of your environment. There is more in your hands to do than just to read. What could that be you might say? Application! Application is the true beauty of whatever information that we have access to- either large or small.

Yes, it is vital that the points discussed in this book are applied, use in your everyday living. If you are waiting for a better time to come when you apply it, unfortunately, it will never happen. Every day has its challenge and difficulty. Therefore, it is now you can create time and work things out the best way possible.

Furthermore, results from the practical suggestions related in this book wouldn't just take effect instantly. Instead, it takes time, though a short time to make it come to a realization. Therefore, you don't expect to start getting results after a few days or reading. But you can be confident that after a few weeks of application, you will surely be stunned at the reward that would come from the application. You will even be astounded to hear comments that are said to commend your ability.

Besides, if you noticed you have symptoms of one or two of the disorder discussed in the final chapter of the book, I'll strongly advise that you don't take it with levity. Instead, take necessary precautions by visiting any medical center to confirm and established the fact. Honestly, though, the earlier you make required investigations, the better for your overall wellbeing.

Avoid conditions and attitude that can negatively affect your memory and brain, which in turn will change how you interact with people out there. Don't forget a well-functioning brain, and memory opens the door for excellent ability to influence people and stay intelligent for the rest of your life!